TO THE MEMORY OF LOUIS WOLCHOVER,
WHO INTERESTED ME IN MANAGEMENT

THE ENTREPRENEURIAL MANAGER

A. L. Minkes is Emeritus Professor of Business Organisation in the University of Birmingham and a Fellow of the Royal Society of Arts. Born in Wales in 1924, he studied Philosophy, Politics and Economics at Balliol College, Oxford, where he gained an M A. He has lectured in universities, management centres in industry, and other organizations, and acted as a consultant on business topics and management training in Britain and overseas. He also spent part of his career with the Economic Commission for Europe of the United Nations.

From 1974 to 1980 he was a non-executive member of the Midlands Postal Board; from 1975 to 1983 he served on the Council of Birmingham Chamber of Industry and Commerce. He has also served on various national and regional committees on management education. Currently a Visiting Professor at the Chinese University of Hong Kong, he is on the Committee on Management and Supervisory Training of the Vocational Training Council in Hong Kong.

He has published widely in books and journals, including *Strategic Management Journal* and the *Journal of General Management*. His books include *An International Census of Manufactures*, *Management Training in Sri Lanka* (with R. M. Withana), and (with C. S. Nuttall) *Business Behaviour and Management Structure*.

Professor Minkes is married with two children.

ENTREPRENEURIAL
MANAGER

DECISIONS, GOALS AND
BUSINESS IDEAS

PENGUIN BOOKS

Penguin Books Ltd, Harmondsworth, Middlesex, England
Viking Penguin Inc., 40 West 23rd Street, New York, New York 10010, U.S.A.
Penguin Books Australia Ltd, Ringwood, Victoria, Australia
Penguin Books Canada Ltd, 2801 John Street, Markham, Ontario, Canada L3R 1B4
Penguin Books (N.Z.) Ltd, 182–190 Wairau Road, Auckland 10, New Zealand

First published 1987
Copyright © A. L. Minkes, 1987
All rights reserved

Made and printed in Great Britain by
Richard Clay Ltd, Bungay, Suffolk
Typeset in Monotype Ehrhardt

1560426

CONTENTS

LIST OF FIGURES

ACKNOWLEDGEMENTS

I am very much indebted to colleagues and students at the University of Birmingham and the Chinese University of Hong Kong, and to managers and administrators in business and other organizations, for many discussions of the ideas in this book. It was written during a period as Visiting Professor at the Chinese University of Hong Kong, which gave me an admirable environment for the purpose.

The illustrative examples come from a variety of sources. Those which refer to Cadbury Schweppes, Tarmac, Thomas Tilling, Manganese Bronze, and Tube Investments are mostly drawn from *Business Behaviour and Management Structure* by A. L. Minkes and C. S. Nuttall (Croom Helm, 1985). Most of the references to the Post Office are based on my experience as a non-executive member of the Midlands Postal Board between 1974 and 1980 and are used by kind permission. Other instances are acknowledged in the appropriate places in the text and notes, but I wish to express general thanks to all those who have been so helpful to me in permitting the use of material. The interpretation of examples and material is, of course, my own.

Professor Gordon Foxall and Dr Simon Vickers read draft manuscripts and made valuable comments; Miss Jody Chan typed successive drafts with patience and skill; and my wife subjected my ideas and their presentation to careful scrutiny.

In the text of the book, I have emphasized the importance of taking responsibility in management. The same principle applies to the author, and for all errors of commission or omission I am, of course, responsible.

A.L.M.

CHAPTER ONE

INTRODUCTION

This book explores a number of ideas, some traditional, some less familiar, which form the basis of the study of management. It has been prompted by concern with the gap which seems to exist between the disciplined presentation in textbooks of such themes as strategy, decision-making, corporate planning, and the reality of the untidy world which managers actually inhabit. There are books which tell the reader what managers do and what they should do. *Should* implies *can*: but the fact that managers do not always follow the prescriptions may mean not that they *refuse to* but that the prescriptions are *not feasible*. But this is not always fully appreciated. Thus, it is admitted that managers cannot have complete knowledge, that they have to operate in conditions of uncertainty, yet they are advised to behave as if they were in a position to evaluate any number of options and to act on their evaluations with complete confidence.

Of course this is not true of everything in the management literature, and there are many writers who focus attention on the real-life situation of managers. Rosemary Stewart's book is aptly entitled *The Reality of Management*; Charles Handy deals directly with real problems in his *Understanding Organizations*. At the level of management skills, there is a good deal of basic material: Robertson and Cooper on *Human Behaviour in Organisations* and W. David Rees on *The Skills of Management* are among recent examples.[1] But especially in the realm of ideas, there is a serious gap. Consider some examples.

In recent years there has been a significant amount of study of strategy formation in the modern business corporation and an increasing interest in the processes and procedures through which decisions are actually made. If a new factory is built, or if a company goes into a new geographical or product market, what are the steps by which the eventual results come about? Who decides and in what ways are the decisions made? If, to take a case which was studied by Witte, a number of organizations decide to buy electronic data-processing equipment, how do they set about it and why do they do so in different ways?[2]

The examples need not be confined to business enterprise. If a university sets up a new medical school or institutes a new degree programme, what are the steps by which intention is translated into fact? How, in other words, is the process managed? To express the question in that way is to suggest that the process is positively and actively managed, that is to say, the organization is not some kind of automated machine but a living community of consciously-deciding individuals. But that in turn leads to the questions: which individuals? and what parts do they play in the total process? Some writers emphasize comprehensive strategic planning: others, like Lindblom and Quinn, in their work on incrementalism (which is discussed in Chapter 4 of this book), suggest that management is a deliberate, *political* process. Like politics, therefore, it is the art of securing consensus and of the possible.

These are questions of practical importance because they have a bearing on what is to be expected of managers and on how, consequently, management education should be developed. If, for example, the Quinn/Lindblom thesis is valid, the study of some form of political science is a good deal more useful for managers than has been commonly supposed. Many of the questions are concerned with the internal workings of the organization, what has been called 'the interior of the black box'. If managers have to work with limited knowledge and under day-to-day pressures, it is important to examine the ways in which they cope and to clarify the ideas which may be useful to them. That is why this book concentrates on management ideas rather than management skills and on stimulating thinking about concepts rather than the acquisition of specific knowledge.

An overall view

The central approach of the book is to consider, in each chapter, an idea or topic which is important to the understanding of management and the manager's tasks. There is no shortage of definitions of management, but while they characteristically, and helpfully, express it as a set of functional activities or relationships, they do not always touch its essence. A human being is made up of many selves and a manager performs many tasks; but what is it that is being done and what is the particular slice of a manager's life which can be classified as management rather than, say, accounting or research, or some other specific function? If, as this book will suggest, management consists in co-ordinating a variety of disciplines, there are very large implications for the qualities and training required of the men and women who become its practitioners. From the outset, this approach implies an understanding of relationships between ideas from different fields and of experts from different disciplines, which has to be based both in behavioural analysis and in the decision sciences.

The introduction of the word 'decision' itself makes explicit that a fundamental aspect of management is the manager's role as a decision-maker. This is now the accepted coinage of books on management; here, the emphasis is on decision-*m*aking rather than decision-*t*aking and on the idea that from a management point of view this is a complex and time-consuming process. The distinction between making and taking is no mere pedantic notion, for it stresses two things. Decisions typically depend on positive action; they have to be made by managers – they do not simply fall unheralded from the skies or a textbook – and it takes time for them to be worked through. Time is crucial in a manager's life, not only because it is a scarce resource on which there are many competing claims, but also because during the passage of time the suppositions on which decisions are based will be altered by changing circumstances. There are many instances of this; among the most interesting are those which are discussed in Chapter 6 in relation to corporate innovation. Thus, for example, there can be very radical differences between the market situation which is envisaged in the early stages in the development of a new product and the situation which is encountered by the time the product is launched.

If all could be foreseen, there would be no problems, indeed no management function to be performed; but it is apparent, in fact, that managers are faced with uncertainty and ambiguity and that they are far removed from an optimizing situation. Does this mean that they cannot behave rationally – that they cannot pursue their predetermined goals? Herbert Simon, whose influence on the development of management thinking and the understanding of administrative systems has been of signal importance, examined particularly the effects on decision-making of the inability of human beings to know enough. He introduced the concept of bounded rationality, the idea that people are rational in a limited definition of that term. They aim at being rational but are limited by their imperfect knowledge. Hence, they satisfice, as he put it, because they are unable to maximize. They settle for solutions which are good enough instead of looking for the best solution. The importance of this concept, whether it is accepted in its entirety or not, is in the light it casts on management in real situations. Faced with the constraints of imperfect knowledge, what can managers do, how can they deal with the problems of decision-making? Much of the work which has been done on the targets at which businesses actually aim – for example, share of the market, acceptable rates of return – stems from the idea that since the best cannot be known and it is impossible to consider every possible option, decision-makers limit the number and kind of the options they are prepared to consider.

This is one of the most important themes considered in this book, for underlying it is the whole question of how managers can come to terms with the pervasive uncertainty of real life, about markets, customers, technology, competitors. Of course the world is not in complete darkness; there is an array of ideas and techniques which provide light for managers. Nevertheless, a major explanation of what managers do and why they do it, why for example firms are often disposed to keep within markets and technologies which are not too remote from their existing knowledge and skills, lies in appreciating the partial ignorance in which decisions have to be made.

It may be, moreover, that explanations of management behaviour in terms of rational models need to be complemented by analysis which sees management as a 'political' activity. One of the puzzles in management experience is the apparent contrast between the obvious need to plan and the scepticism about corporate planning. Many top executives express this scepticism about global planning, especially about what they call 'number crunching', that is to say, plans with large amounts of seemingly precise quantitative data. This attitude lends especial interest to the idea that decision-making, both in the business corporation and in public administration, is incrementalist in character. This presents a step-by-step approach, in contrast to the notion of comprehensive corporate planning. Management is envisaged as a process in which skilful managers actively develop consensus and commitment: the movement of an organization, business or otherwise, is the result of a conscious attempt by managers to bring together divergent interests and perceptions so as to arrive at effective decisions on what to do which are acceptable to the participants.

This concept of management behaviour is itself bound up with the idea of the business enterprise as a system of governance. The modern business corporation is often large and diversified, geographically dispersed and organizationally complex. It has some of the features of a constitutional system with formal rules and procedures and informal conventions of government. In such an organization, there are different objectives, differences which are inherent in the existence of the different individuals, groups, and departments of which it is composed. The task of management is not to ignore or to try to think away the differences and conflicts of view and interests, but to arrive at a course of action in spite of them. Thus, management has some of the characteristics of a (small 'p') political activity in which leadership, persuasion, negotiation, trust, are significant elements. These ideas are discussed in greater detail throughout this book because of the bearing they have on what management is and what qualities are required in managers.

In the midst of concern with organization and the processes and procedures of decision-making, especially in the large and complex modern corporation, it is vital not to lose sight of the function of the individual manager and of the entrepreneurial role. That means the role of the manager as innovator, not only in respect of new products and markets, but also of organizational change. The dynamics of innovation are by no means fully understood, but there is an increasing volume of work on, for example, the distinction between big innovative jumps and the more modest ventures into neighbouring fields which are often characteristic of large businesses.

One of the most interesting and important features of management, particularly but not only in large organizations, is the interplay between individual and organization, between entrepreneurial leadership and bureaucratic process. Nowhere is this more critical than in the areas of strategy and planning. The first is fundamental, since the strategic decisions in an enterprise will determine its pattern of products and markets and its corporate structure. Decisions about the product-market mix will carry with them a portfolio of consequential decisions, on finance, forms of growth, and so on. So what is business strategy and how does it emerge in the modern corporation? One of the points which is stressed in this book is that while it is true that the structure of an organization may be determined by its strategy, it is also true that the structure of an organization may govern strategy. In other words, the way a business is organized will influence not only the efficiency with which it accomplishes its tasks but also the choice of tasks to be done, because it will influence what the managers see as its opportunities. This leads naturally to the idea of planning in an enterprise: what is involved in planning and who should do it? What, if any, is the relation between business planning and creative business behaviour? For although there is scepticism about planning and planners, there is clearly a place for them and for managers themselves in the planning process.

All the themes which are here discussed can be readily perceived in the context of business and the market as a test of effective decision-making. But management and the need for managers are not at all confined to business enterprise, and writers and practitioners are grappling with problems in non-profit and non-market organizations and some which are only partially market-based. In some respects, the experience of nationalized industries is instructive as an example of the management questions which arise when enterprises are required to respond both to the forces of the market and of government. In a sense, this can be regarded as a special case of a general problem of ambiguity and duality of the criteria against which management performance has to be assessed. Thus, in hospitals and universities, organizations which are frequently what Drucker terms 'budget-based', the mix of objectives and the tensions between administrators and professional experts, such as doctors and academics, present distinctive difficulties in management. How far these are specific to organizations of this type is a matter for debate: it is certainly true that the same or similar problems are found in business enterprises, for example in their research and personnel departments, which are not directly involved in the market for products. But in non-market and non-profit organizations they have a special significance because they influence the character of the organizations as a whole.

Insights and guidelines

It can be seen, then, that this book deals with concepts which are among the major components in management knowledge and expertise, although it clearly does not attempt to explore each of them in all its historical ramifications or to produce in the end a single set of comprehensive generalizations. The ideas are interdependent, yet in a sense each chapter stands on its own.

It sets out, instead, to do three things. The first is to focus attention on *ideas*, in pursuit of the proposition that management is an intellectual challenge. The second is to suggest that, although no universal theory is propounded (on the principle that a unitary theory would by that very token be wrong), it is possible to trace out general insights, recurring themes, and common threads, and to suggest a number of helpful generalizations. Lastly, by interspersing a profusion of examples and illustrations, it will show how the ideas in each chapter are relevant to the understanding of management as a practice.

What are some of the common threads? That management provides an intellectual challenge, banal though it may seem to say it, is one thread and worthy of notice if only because the words 'intellectual' and 'academic' are sometimes given a pejorative ring. Another important theme is that the management of enterprises is an interplay between individual and organization. Even in the seemingly bureaucratic large-scale organization of so many modern businesses, the entrepreneur is not dead and the spirit of entrepreneurship is not irrelevant. With all the development of management techniques, the qualities of initiative and judgement, of alertness and creativity, remain at the heart of business behaviour. But they are exercised within a framework of organizational process and procedure which the effective manager has to learn to understand and to utilize.

Some of these topics are extensively discussed in the literature of management studies; others appear in advanced books and in academic journals but have not yet found their way into the basic textbooks which are used in introductory courses on principles of management. There seems no good reason why these ideas should not be released from the box.

CHAPTER TWO

WHAT IS MANAGEMENT ALL ABOUT?

What is management itself? What does it mean, and what are the tasks and qualities which are required of managers?

There are three ways of looking at this topic. The first might be called the conventional way of examining definitions of the kind which many books consider. The second is concerned with the reality of the manager's day, the fragmented life and varied pressures which are the regular experience. The third approach is to analyse management as an idea – what it is that managers are doing when they are engaged in management. This focuses not on the specific functions they perform but on the inherent nature of management activity.

On definitions of management

Definitions can serve several purposes. They tell the reader what the subject means, or at least what the author means by it. In this way, they mark out the area of discussion, influence the method of approach to a subject, and simultaneously indicate what is *not* included within it. This can be extremely important; think of the following examples drawn from economics.

In 1932 the late Lord Robbins published his famous book *An Essay on the Nature and Significance of Economic Science*, in which he defined economics as a science which studied the allocation between competing ends of scarce resources which have alternative uses. This definition greatly influenced many economists and the way the subject was studied, because it focused attention on relative scarcity and on prices. That is quite different from studying economics as, say, the history and structure of economic institutions. Jacob Viner said that 'economics is what economists do': and Keynes, in his introduction to the *Cambridge Economic Handbook Series* (1922), characterized the theory of economics as a method, 'a technique of thinking'. This way of looking at the subject inclines economists towards the construction of analytical models rather than the empirical study of behaviour in organizations.

Similarly with management: some definitions emphasize the element of co-ordination of resources, others the task of managing people. For some writers, the elements of leadership and direction hold the centre of the stage; for others, planning and control are the crucial features.

So what can be picked out as characteristics of management in the profusion of definitions?

1. A first and striking feature of management is that it exists essentially because of the existence of organizations. Of course it is true that individuals are said to manage their affairs, personal, financial, and career: an individual may 'manage' his investment portfolio or his estate, and a one-man business, which can hardly be said to be an organization, can be said to require managing. But this is a rather superficial use of the term 'management', which means no more than to say that men and women have to look after their business matters and personal concerns. When they are members of organizations, as when they are employed in a firm, their arrangements are part of a network which involves other people, perhaps in very large numbers.

This may seem so obvious as to be hardly worth saying: managers must be very well aware of this. But it is worth emphasizing for a number of reasons. A manager is not a Robinson Crusoe: he does not carry on his activities or make his decisions on his own. Herbert Simon put it in this way, that when an executive makes a decision, he does so with one eye on the matter in hand and one eye on its organizational consequences.[1] Managers know, in other words, that what they do affects other members of the organization and they in turn are affected by the actions of others. Thus management involves a relationship of interdependence, in all kinds of ways. Decisions about production involve requirements for the purchase of materials or components; the transfer of staff from one task to another creates the need to consider the vacancies it causes.

Just as managers are not isolated individuals, so their actions are not isolated incidents, and management requires, therefore, an awareness of a whole set of interrelationships. The study of management is partly the study of managerial action, but it is also the study of how that action is generated and processed in the framework of organization.

2. A second feature is that management is about the genesis and progress of change. In a totally unchanging world, there would be no requirement for management at all. When people say that there is a problem of managing change, they are in a sense understating matters, because management *is about* change. One way of expressing it is to say that in an unchanging world there would only be the administrative task of keeping things going, of administering established routines and procedures. Suppose, for example, that a large retail organization has an established system allowing customers to return articles which they have purchased and which turn out not to be suitable. Marks and Spencer do this: clothing bought in any of their stores can be returned to any other of their stores throughout Britain. The rules which Marks and Spencer apply in this respect are well-known and long-established. A store manager may doubtless exercise discretion in borderline cases, but the procedure appears to be quite standard. This is fundamentally a matter of administration.

Consider another instance: a group of civil servants in a very closely regulated, partly legally-based department (overseas) were discussing with a visiting academic the possibility of running a series of management seminars for the staff. The academic visitor asked some of them what their work consisted of, and they replied 'We administer the ordinances.' Since they claimed that they had no discretion in interpreting the ordinances and when in doubt 'We consult a senior officer', he concluded that they had explicit administrative tasks but they had not shown him that they exercised a managerial function. Once again, this was a matter of administration.

At what point could these examples be translated into a management situation? When a business is considering whether or not to *change* its procedures, or when, as in the case of the civil servants, the discussion turned to possible *changes* in the organization of their department, management questions were bound to arise. These are quite modest examples of changes, which serve to show, nevertheless, that a transition from administration to management occurs as soon as questions are raised of the type: what procedures should we institute, what new rules are appropriate, what new methods are appropriate? These are management questions: it is only when they have been answered and decisions have been made about them that the task of administering the rules can begin.

Of course, the point has been exaggerated for the sake of exposition: the distinction between management and administration is not always perfectly clear and precise. But the principle is valid.

3. An important approach to definitions of management is that it involves working through other people. The work of managers requires them to organize others: they have to allocate tasks to subordinates and to supervise and control the results. One consequence is that managers are dependent on the skills and performance of other people, and, interestingly enough, this is more significant the higher up the management chain they are. The apex of the pyramid ultimately rests on its base. In a sense, therefore, to be at the top of the organization means both to be in a position of authority and to be in a position of dependence. The balance between authority, and the power conferred by it, and reliance on others will vary from one business to another, depending on their size, managerial style, cultural traditions, and so on. But companies do recognize this factor. For example, John Neville, who was chief executive of Manganese Bronze, spoke of the relationship between the group headquarters and the subsidiaries as one in which the centre had to rely on the ability of the senior executives in the subsidiaries. It had to trust them; and the word *trust* was used explicitly by Sir Patrick Meaney, who was chief executive of Thomas Tilling,[2] and Gordon Yardley, managing director of its subsidiary company Newey and Eyre, to describe the relationship between them. In turn, Yardley saw his relationship with his subordinates in the same light: he expressed it by saying that when he

planned a visit to a branch of his company, he checked first with the branch manager that it was acceptable. This picture of dependence does not imply absence of authority and power. The same John Neville made it clear that the subsidiary had to deliver the goods: if not, the company could replace the senior executives with others who would do the job. What this means is that choosing people in whom reliance can be placed, who can be _depended on_, in other words, is a critical task in management. But this dependence which comes from working through other people has two other substantial consequences. One is that management has a waiting aspect; managers spend part of their time waiting for the results of tasks which they have delegated to others. The other, and more important, consequence is that management means taking responsibility for the activities of others. In a marvellous and courageous passage in his history of _The Second World War_, Winston Churchill comments as follows about his horrified discovery that Singapore, far from being a fortress, was acutely vulnerable to land-based attack: 'I ought to have known. My advisers ought to have known and I ought to have been told, and I ought to have asked.'[3]

Churchill was here emphasizing the doctrine of ultimate responsibility – where the buck stops – and it is a lesson which can be applied at all levels of management where managers are concerned with the work of others who report to them. How this responsibility can be honoured and by what means of control, formal and informal, managers can reconcile the burden of responsibility with the delegation of tasks to others (who cannot be supervised every moment of the day) is one of the major management questions in the modern business corporation.

4. Since management is concerned with change, it can be seen to have an entrepreneurial as well as an administrative aspect. There is a good deal of debate about the meaning of the term 'entrepreneur', but for the purposes of this chapter entrepreneurship is taken to be concerned with three things:

    (a) determination of the mission or basic direction of the enterprise;

    (b) choice of strategy for effecting the business purposes;

(c)   creation of the corporate structure, i.e. the organizational means for devising and implementing strategy.

Thus Sir Adrian Cadbury in defining the strategic characteristics of Cadbury Schweppes made this series of statements. At one time, before the merger with Schweppes, Cadburys' business could have been defined in terms of its basic raw material, the cocoa bean. Now it could be classified as the supply of snack foods of which it happens that many are covered with chocolate: since, furthermore, the company is essentially a marketing concern, it can be defined in the context of its distribution outlets, e.g. supermarkets.

Similarly, Robin Martin, who, at the head of Tarmac, presided over its development into a major construction company, categorized it within construction and civil engineering, a view which top direction of the company continued to hold. In going on to strategic choice, Martin spoke particularly of diversification, within that context, as a means of fostering growth.

Concern with 'mission' and 'strategic choice' must lie with managers; with whom else? With which managers and at which levels of the organization are other matters, which belong to later chapters. That they are part of management responsibility is crucial, since from this idea flows a whole set of commitments and tasks, and a picture of what constitutes an effective manager.

The third point mentioned above was the creation of the organization. Professor Ansoff has pointed out that in traditional economic theory the manager was perceived as what he calls 'an operator of a fixed arm'.[4] By this he meant that the manager was regarded as somebody who took a set of inputs (labour, materials, equipment) and used them in the 'best' combination so as to produce output at minimum cost. In reality, however, a large part of management is concerned with the design and establishment of the structure of the organization. As will be seen later in this book, the formation of strategy is an abstract exercise without the organizational means of making it effective. Textbooks of management rightly concentrate attention on the importance of organization, and this is not a 'given': it has to be designed and created. In a very large company with numerous departments and divisions this may seem obvious, but it is interesting that management has to face this task even when the business is of quite modest size. The British industrialist John Crabtree emphasized this point in an unpublished manuscript describing the growth of his firm, which made electrical products, from its inception with 'a man and a boy' in 1921 to about 1,000 employees in 1935, when he died. He thought that organizations did not grow 'naturally' and that at successive increments of two or three hundred employees, management needed to consider how to reconstruct the ways in which it handled its tasks.[5]

On the manager's working day

In a conversation with the author a number of years ago, Professor Bela Gold remarked that at the University of Pittsburgh it had been his custom to take graduate students downtown to observe for themselves how executives actually spent their time. He thought it might disabuse them of the notion that executives sat back in order to brood on long-term strategic developments: it could be that in fact they were struggling to keep the in-tray from overflowing.

The daily life of the manager is filled with specific tasks and current pressures. The managing director of a large British company, when asked how he felt that industrial management differed from academic life, replied that he thought it much more *fragmented*. 'I do not find it difficult,' he said, 'to find a spare hour to devote to one job, but I find it extremely difficult to find two successive hours.'

Curzon gives a very apt example of a manager's working day, illustrating an imaginary but realistic factory manager responsible to the company's managing director. His engagement diary records his anticipated arrangements:

0845   Deal with day's correspondence
0915   Meeting with R & D departmental head: discussion on delay in presentation of new design
0930   Meeting with union representative: grievances concerning new shift system
1000   Tour of loading bays: observation of procedures
1030   Meeting with departmental heads: discussion of preliminary estimates for next financial year
1145   Work on preparation of preliminary estimates document

1230   Working lunch with industrial editor of national newspaper
1345   Further tour of loading bays
1415   Further preparation of estimates document
1515   Meeting with ... overseas marketing manager: discussion on developments in SE Asian markets.

Curzon goes on to comment:

In the event, the 0930 meeting continues until 1030, and preparation of the estimates document, programmed for 1145, is abandoned in favour of an emergency meeting with factory shop stewards, designed to head off a conflict concerning the allocation of overtime. Throughout [his] day he is involved in the processes of communication, e.g. listening, observing, ordering, persuading, writing.[6]

These passages are used by Curzon to stress the manager's role in 'the processes of communication', but they also serve to underline four critical aspects of management life. The first, as has already been suggested, is its *fragmentation* and the short time which can be given to individual important topics. The second is the *variety* of matters which come before the manager's attention: new design, union grievance, loading bay procedures, estimates, working lunch with journalist, overseas markets. Thirdly, there is the variety of *people* with whom he is involved: departmental heads, union representative, journalist, company marketing manager. Lastly, there is the problem of *delay and interruptions* – the extended 0930 meeting, and the emergency meeting which leads him to defer the preparation of the estimates document, very important job though that must clearly be. And if the experience of being dean of a faculty in a university is any guideline, there are other interruptions: for example, the telephone, the indispensable deadly instrument, and the sheer amount of time it takes to get from one place to another.

It is not surprising, therefore, that writers like Handy should lay stress on the manager's problem of living 'in two or more time dimensions':

The manager is, above all, responsible for the future ...
But this management of the future has to go hand in hand with the responsibility for the present ... It is not easy to live in two or more time dimensions at once. It is hard to plan creatively for five years hence with a

redundancy interview scheduled for one hour's time. Just as routine drives out non-routine, so the present can easily obliterate the future. By concentrating on the problems of the present the future becomes in its turn a series of present problems or crises, intervention by the manager in a power role becomes legitimate, even essential, there is still less time available for the future, the manager feels indispensable and legitimized by crisis. The cycle has become self-fulfilling. *Unless the manager is able to live successfully in two time dimensions he will make the present more difficult than it need be and will unsuccessfully manage the future.*[7] [Italics added]

This passage has been quoted at length because it forms a whole and poses the well-known problem of reconciling attention to present pressures with the need to attend to future concerns. This is not something which is confined to middle managers. Sir Isaac Wolfson, asked at a University of Birmingham seminar if running so large a business as Great Universal Stores did not give him ulcers, replied – jestingly, it is true – 'No: they are for middle managers.' But even top managers face the problem of fragmentation and variety of specific problems. It is not difficult to find examples, and those which follow, from the experience of the Midlands Postal Region in Britain, illustrate the point. Senior management could not spend all its time thinking about long-term strategic plans. It had to consider a range of individual topics.

As the mechanization of letter sorting offices advanced, the prospect arose in 1978–9 that, except for early morning mail, the 'Stratford-upon-Avon' postmark would disappear, to be replaced by 'Coventry' or a generic title. A simple enough matter of efficiency, it might be thought, but in fact a complicated, quite time-consuming affair which engaged attention at senior level. The local MP, district councillors and many local bodies, headed by the Shakespeare Birthplace Trust, lobbied fiercely to retain the Stratford postmark. They argued that it was regarded by overseas tourists, on whom Stratford depends so much for its prosperity, as an important feature for which 'Coventry' was no substitute at all. Hence, the simple matter of efficiency turned out to be sufficiently significant to engage attention at the highest Post Office level (with the additional complication that in a public corporation political pressure is more difficult to resist). Or again, a postal business will be seriously affected by the availability and punctuality of the railway service, and any deficiencies may cause short-run crises as well as long-term policy problems. Machinery breakdown or industrial disputes with engineers assume a significance in the context of mechanization which can result in an engagements diary very like the hypothetical one outlined by Curzon.

One more example from the postal business deserves to be cited because it illustrates so well the 'localized', specific problems which can occupy the time of managers. The business is labour-intensive, i.e. it has a relatively high input of labour, by contrast with telecommunications. It also involves an important element of what are called unsocial hours, because postal employees who make early morning deliveries of letters have to arrive very early at the sorting offices in preparation for their delivery 'walk'. Scrupulous though the Post Office may be in explaining this to young recruits to the business, the experience sometimes comes as an unpalatable shock in the dark early hours of winter, and some of them leave within a fairly short time. This creates problems for the business, and hence occupies the attention of managers, both in respect of supply of labour and of the cost of the training which has been invested in personnel and which has to be repeated for the replacement intake.

This chapter has given much attention to specific examples: they are certainly particular, but they are also typical. They are not intended to prove that managers are rushed off their feet all the time, that the pressure is unrelenting, and that time is an inexorable enemy of even a single long-term thought. But they lend practical force to the view expressed in the passage from Handy cited above, and they oblige managers to consider how to secure that life in two dimensions which he regards as essential if they are to perform successfully. That is why companies quite often try to devise means by which their managers can be got away from day-to-day pressures. They may use special 'think tank' gatherings away from the office, 'brainstorming sessions', seminars, project groups: they may provide for occasions and facilities to encourage informal exchange of ideas.

The concept of management

So far in this chapter, the implications of some characteristic definitions of management have been considered and some picture of the managerial day has been given. In this penultimate section, the purpose is to analyse the *nature* of management as an idea. In any organization, be it business or otherwise, men and women play many parts: each individual may play more than one part. The finance director of a company will have regard to financial matters and will also contribute to wider policy discussions on the board of directors of the enterprise. A manager may be engaged in some specific function and also be managing a department. The question to be examined now is: what is it that is being done which can properly be called *management*?

Consider an example. Suppose that a young man or woman has graduated from a university with a degree in chemistry and has found a job in the research and development department of a business enterprise. And suppose that he or she is put to work on the chemical properties of the materials which the company utilizes. Clearly such a person cannot be said to be engaged in *management*, since, whatever the formal status in the company, the work is that of a chemist – much as it might be if the same person were working in, say, a university laboratory.

Now suppose that the chemist is promoted to be head of the R & D department. It appears to become immediately obvious that the kind of work – *or a significant part of it* – can legitimately be classified as management. Why is this so?

1. In the first place, it is virtually certain that there will no longer be as much time for chemistry and, particularly, for keeping up to date with fresh developments in the subject. Of course this will partly depend on the size of the department: the bigger and more varied its activities, the stronger the argument. (Similar circumstances are experienced by academics who assume significant administrative responsibilities.)

2. The kinds of decision with which the new head of the department is now concerned are quite different. Imagine that the department

has been allocated a fixed budget of £x thousand, that it has ten chemically feasible projects in hand, and that to persist with all of them would exceed the budget. The head must accordingly either persuade higher management to increase the budget allocation or pare down the ten projects to, say, the *best* eight. But the criteria for choosing and the language in which the case will be argued will be economic, commercial, market criteria. Interested though the company may be in the inherent intellectual quality of the ideas which are generated in its research laboratories, its budget allocations must be judged against the contribution those ideas will ultimately make to the 'bottom line', the profit account of the company.

Or consider again:

3. As head of department, the manager has to think about a variety of staff questions. Colleagues whose projects do not receive what they regard as adequate funding may feel aggrieved. Then there will be matters of recruitment and promotion of staff to consider and questions of how to balance individual talents with organizational harmony. This requires an understanding, once again, of factors other than the chemistry of research products; it requires, rather, the chemistry of organization and human relations, of personnel and social psychology.

This analysis suggests that the transition into management is a movement *from specialist to generalist*. Beginning as a specialist in chemistry, working strictly within that discipline, the chemist has now to be concerned with a range of activities and decisions. This means co-ordinating variables from a variety of disciplines in which it is virtually certain that this particular individual is *not* expert and in which the company does employ experts. Thus, all management can be regarded as *general* management: the phrase 'specialist management' is a contradiction in terms.

Is this an exaggerated picture of the idea of management? Is it an excessively academic view? Is it not at variance with the earlier sections of this chapter which show the manager as a busy, practical person? Do managers sit back and analyse problems in terms of economics, sociology, and social psychology? Not everybody goes into business with a specialist training in chemistry or accounting or anything else with immediate applicability to a particular aspect of a company's activity. Graduates in English, history, geography, and young men and women who are not graduates at all take jobs in industry and commerce: on the other hand, many entrants have degrees or diplomas in business studies, so that they are quite well-equipped in the relevant disciplines. And even if the analysis is valid, is it not applicable mainly to large and bureaucratic business corporations?

It is true that the story of the chemist is hypothetical and simplified, that it is chosen partly to make a point: but that does not mean that it fails to get at the essence of management. Suppose, for example, that the head of the R & D department is promoted further so that the career progress looks as follows:

R & D department

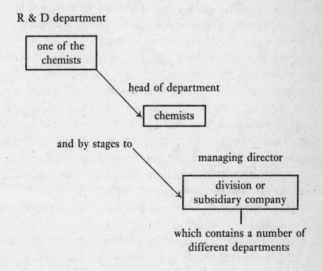

Thus, the further that managers advance, the less can they be seen in a specialist function; and the more departments which fall within their ultimate responsibility, the more evident it becomes that their decisions are generalist and interdisciplinary in character. Although it is perfectly true, therefore, that managers perform specific tasks within specific functional areas of a company, it is also true that the peculiar characteristic of management as an idea lies in its generalist nature. Sometimes, in fact, this is expressed in the title 'general manager', given to managers responsible for an area or division in which they are concerned with a number of departmental functions.

Some implications and conclusions

The first implication which may be drawn from the foregoing analysis is by way of being a puzzle or a paradox. On the one hand, there has been a striking increase in the number of 'expertises' and experts. Once upon a time, men spoke of the Renaissance man as the ideal, with a wide-ranging culture, and of the generalist, grounded perhaps in the classics, as the most appropriate man for top-level administration. But nowadays many subjects which once filled a single textbook have opened up into numbers of separate specialisms: there are accountants and tax accountants, lawyers and company lawyers, systems analysts and computer programmers. How is this compatible with the view that management is general management?

It means, first of all, that the task of management is more complex than in the past, because the number of special fields which are relevant to ultimate decisions is larger and the element of expertise is greater. This means, secondly, that the kind of general training which is suitable for development of managers has also changed, as was already pointed out in 1963 by the Franks Report on *British Business Schools*.[8] This training, whether in formal education or through experience, is more likely to turn on business subjects, but not on any single discipline.

A second implication concerns the problem of promotion in management life. If management is general – so that the head of a police force need not have been a policeman or the head of a postal business a postman – what are the advantages and disadvantages of bringing in managers from outside a company? This question is especially acute in organizations which have a high professional content: hospitals, social work departments, schools, colleges and universities. But they also exist in business. For example, if a company appoints a new sales director, what kind of background is essential or simply desirable?

The late Sir Frederick Hooper, who was managing director of Schweppes (a considerable time before its merger with Cadbury), once described how, after looking at a number of candidates who had come up through the sales function, the company eventually chose as director a man from production. He had the qualities of understanding data and handling organization which outweighed his inexperience in the field of sales.

This anecdote is not a universal recommendation, and choices of this kind may raise very difficult problems within an organization. But it illustrates the point about general management and the practical difficulty that can arise in finding suitable general managers in a world where recruits enter on employment in a specific function.

There is a third aspect, which is concerned with what a business enterprise is required to do. In Professor Drucker's view, it exists essentially to supply products to consumers, who have to be willing to pay for them: this is the primary test of its performance and the measure of its success. He particularly, and other writers too, see business management, therefore, as an economic instrument, using economic resources to generate wealth and the power to create wealth. Management derives what Drucker calls its authority from its ability to meet customer demand at the relevant prices, and everything that managers do and all the decisions they make must be assessed against the test of economic performance. This means that the ability to identify where the market lies, to decide who the customer is, and to know how to satisfy wants, are inherent in the management task.[9]

Even in a non-business, non-market situation, decisions have to be made about what are the right things to supply and how they can be most efficiently supplied. But the task of actually managing a complex organization, business or non-business, requires, as Drucker himself appreciates, a variety of skills and activities. The ultimate test may be economic performance but the management tasks cannot be defined solely in terms of economics. If there were a single 'bottom line' for every management activity and decision, life would be immeasurably easier for managers: but there is not. Rosemary Stewart, who says that since 'Managers' jobs vary so much' she doubted 'the truth of the common statement "a good manager can manage anything"', adds:

We quoted Sune Carlson's pioneering study of nine managing directors and subsequent studies, which show that typically the manager's day is a very fragmented one. This makes it harder to organize one's time effectively. Research has shown that *many managers require political skills* as well as the, more commonly emphasized, supervisory skills.[10] [Italics added]

Two further implications may be drawn from the argument of this chapter. One is that a considerable part of the management task is concerned with the *internal environment* of the organization. Managers certainly have to be alert to the external environment, of customers, competitors, technology, government: without that they would be lost. But a great deal of their work centres round internal management: organizational design, committee or board meetings, discussions with other managers about personnel, and generally, in fact, maintaining the health of the organization and ensuring its innovative development.

The other implication is that management is an integrative activity. One of the most forceful expressions of this view is made by Professor Kanter, who distinguishes organizations which are integrative and see problems as wholes from those which work by what she terms 'walling off a piece of experience and preventing it from being touched or affected by any new experiences.'[11] She emphasizes a point which has been of basic importance in this chapter, that management requires the co-ordination of a variety of specialists, each with an approach to problems which reflects a specific background and training. The strength of an organization resides in its diversity, but, of course, the point is to bring together the diverse views so as to arrive at agreed courses of action. Within an organization, an integrative approach which avoids 'walling off' means that ideas can move across internal, departmental frontiers, and that innovative practices can challenge the old and generate change.

Professor Kanter contrasts this approach with what she terms 'segmentalism', which 'assumes that problems can be solved when they are carved into pieces and the pieces are assigned to specialists who work in isolation.' This is another issue: to the extent, however, that it emphasizes the significance of integrating specialisms, it underlines a central point of this chapter.

CHAPTER THREE

DECISIONS AND DECISION-MAKING

Decisions and the process of decision-making as a purposive activity which is at the heart of the manager's task have come to occupy a central place in the study of management. There is now a substantial volume of work on the meaning of decision – what is really involved in the idea – and of empirical evidence on how decisions are in practice made in organizations. Some of this work is primarily concerned with general classification and instances; some, of which Witte's study mentioned earlier is an interesting example, is more closely concerned with the detailed processes or stages in which decision-makers become engaged in specific cases.

On the idea of decision: some general propositions

Many students are first introduced to the word 'decision' in the framework of economics and so learn, early on, a useful if highly simplified catechism of the following kind:

> A decision means a choice, and a choice implies that there are at least two possible courses of action. When the hero in the western film says 'I guess you have no choice', he is also saying, in effect, 'There is no decision to be made.'
>
> All decisions can be looked at as costs, since the choice of any one option involves the forgoing of the others; more specifically, sacrificing the next best.
>
> This is the famous doctrine of economics that costs are opportunity costs, i.e. that the true cost of any choice is the next best alternative which has been forgone.

If an organization could be expressed, so to speak, as a picture on an X-ray plate, what would appear would be a network of interrelated individual decisions. Those decisions would represent choices which had been made, options discarded, and hence opportunity costs incurred. This way of looking at decisions and costs has four clear advantages:

1. It emphasizes that a decision is a commitment to a course of action.

2. It shows that each decision has both its positive and negative sides: the choice of option A means forgoing option B . . .

3. Decisions appear as concerns with the future: in economist's language, 'Bygones are forever bygones.' Nobody can decide what to do in the past: decisions are made presently with consequences which flow in the future.

4. Since decision is a choice of one commitment as against others, it is concerned with change.

This picture displays nothing, however, of how decisions are actually made; indeed, it is not intended to do so. As a matter of fact, the conventional textbook of economics treats the decision-maker as a wholly rational being with full knowledge of future costs and prices. But if the decision-makers have this perfect knowledge, 'don't have problems with memory loss or memory recall',[1] they really do not have decisions to make at all. A primary point for management is that decisions have to be made precisely because managers do not have perfect knowledge: to assume such knowledge is to assume away both the management problem and the need for managers.

This rather theoretical point can be explored further. In reality, everybody will agree that the future is unknown: still more important is the consideration that the future is *unknowable*, that is to say, there are events which will occur one day, products which will appear on the market, which cannot be inferred from past experience. Even if development has reached a stage where the nature of a new product or technological change can be specified, the effect in the market for any particular firm is not fully knowable. Some simple examples will illustrate the point: the use of PVC for rainwater pipes instead of cast iron, the introduction of plastic in a variety of uses, of water-based emulsion paints, of the jet engine in aircraft, have radically altered market environments. Change in a general sense can be foreseen but its specific direction cannot. Professor Shackle, in fact, in his work as an economist on the creative aspect of entrepreneurship, saw decisions about the future as the creation of the future rather than its discovery.

Of course all this is partly a matter of balance. An individual who decides to buy another bar of chocolate is pretty sure that it will be enjoyable, because it is possible to call on previous experience. Similarly, a shopkeeper who stocks a particular line will feel safe in replenishing it because of the track record of its sales. A company which agrees to pay an annuity to an elderly client can look at its actuarial tables: it knows that not all its annuitants will live to be centenarians. In other words, there is a mixture of reasonable likelihood, informed guesswork, and established probabilities in many cases, even if there cannot be utter certainty. But a shopkeeper who decides to carry a line he has never hitherto attempted to sell, or to open in a location of which he has no previous direct experience, is moving into somewhat darker terrain. For one who introduces a product which has never previously been on the market, the argument applies yet more strongly.

The significant point in management terms is that it is precisely the uncertainties which require managers to make decisions. If they knew, absolutely, they would have absolutely nothing to decide. But their lack of knowledge, the partial ignorance in which they must necessarily operate, obliges them to make choices. And, as Terence Hutchison puts it, 'as soon as one cannot, or does not, continue to assume that people make the single "right" maximizing decision, one has to discover and justify the particular decision which they will make of the virtually infinite number of "wrong" ones.'[2]

This calls to mind the remark of Sir Harry Jephcott, who was chairman of the pharmaceuticals firm Glaxo; asked at a seminar to say something about wrong decisions which had been made in the company (instead of only giving right ones), he replied: 'Do you mean those which were 51 per cent wrong/49 per cent right instead of

51 per cent right/49 per cent wrong?' The very fact that one choice has explicitly or implicitly displaced another, the consequences of which may now never be fully known, means that decision-makers are always leaving behind them forks in the road leading to possibilities they may now never be able to evaluate.

On the idea of decision-making

The phrase decision-*m*aking, rather than decision-*t*aking, is chosen deliberately for the following reasons. One is simply the growing use of the term in the literature of administration and management. Writing in 1965 that 'decision-making concepts have become highly popular in writing about administration', Herbert Simon commented on the extent to which the term decision-making occurred in the journal *Public Administration*, from three occasions in the titles of articles in the first fifteen volumes to ten instances in the next eight.[3] Looking, furthermore, at the tools available for decision-making at that time, and even now, it is evident that there has been a striking growth in quantitative methods and techniques. Operations research and management science have developed powerful instruments; linear programming, queuing theory, inventory models, and other mathematical techniques have come greatly to the fore. Simon remarks that 'myriads of arithmetic calculations are carried out routinely in many business and governmental organizations to reach the actual decisions from day to day.'[4] Mathematical sophistication, though it is true that it evokes scepticism and criticism, is clearly significant, and the computer has emerged as an everyday force in the decision process.

Innumerable job advertisements and business school courses in quantitative methods underscore this comment, and just as in any physical activity, tools and equipment are used for making things, so the existence of tools of management enhances the idea that decisions are *made*. In contrast to the use of the word *taken*, with its connotation of a snapshot at one instant of time, this tends to underline the idea that decisions are manufactured with decision-making aids.

A second, quite fundamental reason for stressing the element of making, is that there is a decision *process*; decision-making is a *pro-*

cessual activity or set of activities. 'A decision', according to Simon, 'is not a simple, unitary event, but the product of a complex social process generally extending over a considerable period of time.'[5] Consider some elements in that process and, to begin with, why a decision should be made at all. Logically speaking, the critical first element in the decision-making process is the recognition that a decision is called for, i.e. that it requires to be made. This may be provoked by a crisis, or it may be the result of a growing accumulation of smaller dissatisfactions with a current state of affairs. A striking example is what can happen to a very successful business like Lesney in Britain, makers of Matchbox toys, which eventually collapsed. At a relatively late stage, the company sought to meet the invasion of its market by competition, by diversifying away from its dependence on die-cast toy cars. In the event, and for a number of reasons, it was *too* late. It is arguable that in this instance it was failure to perceive that there was a problem looming ahead which caused postponement of the recognition that a decision was required.

A less drastic but equally pertinent example was given by Crabtree, the industrialist referred to in Chapter 2. When the number of employees in his firm had reached 550,

the anomalous situation had arisen that while production had greatly increased, too much of the product had gone into stock and too little was being actually sent out to customers; as a consequence, customer-complaints were becoming serious. Moreover, the situation was financially disastrous, as the growth of stock represented a drain on cash, and the potential income was not being realised. [Thus, in Crabtree's words] The organisation we had initiated around the 300 [employees] mark was not functioning satisfactorily. It was piling up stock, but it wasn't getting it out.[6]

The rise in customer complaints generated in Crabtree's mind the conviction that decisions were required about the *organization of the business*. It was necessary to perceive not only that it was time for decisions but also what those decisions should be about. In this instance, Crabtree concluded that this was not a matter of minor corrections or emollient correspondence with customers. It was a matter of recognizing that the organization which had once been appropriate had ceased to fit the circumstances.

Just as there is a critical first element in decision-making, so there are end stages. A decision is meaningless if nothing is implemented. To say 'I have decided to buy a car' and then not to buy one is not a decision to buy a car: it is either a decision subsequently cancelled by another one, i.e. a change of mind, or it is a decision to make a statement. A decision is part of a process which includes implementation, and even that is not the end of the story. When a decision is carried through, a whole set of other decisions will be involved, e.g. if a new factory is to be erected, who will build it and where? Since there is always the likelihood that things will not turn out as anticipated and since there is the need for control of the activities, the process must include feedback, monitoring, review, and adaptation. The consequences of some decisions, indeed, may go on almost indefinitely, like the ripples from a stone dropped in a pool, with successive decisions stemming from the initial stage.

There is a third reason for using the term decision-making, which is that it draws attention to the fact that managers have a positive decisional role. Mintzberg, in a slightly different context, makes a number of points which are apposite in the present argument. His emphasis is on the manager as 'the formal authority' whose prerogative it is to make decisions for his unit and who is in fact the only person equipped to exercise it. Decisions are commitments to action and may involve new departures. The manager is the 'nerve center' of his unit and, Mintzberg contends, 'only he has the full and current information to make the set of decisions that determines the unit's strategy.'[7]

The terminology of that quotation is open to criticism – 'nerve center' and 'full and current information' are strong words. But the implication conveyed of a decision-maker is an important one and it can be reinforced by another point. Some decisions, perhaps many, are made in response to signals, much as braking in a motor car is a response to a red traffic signal, or, less automatically, adjustment in prices or advertising budgets is a response to changes in sales volume. These are reactive decisions: but there are also what are called proactive decisions, in which managers are consciously looking for opportunities to make decisions.

To round off these analytical points, it is convenient to turn once again to Herbert Simon who has pioneered so much work on decision-making, and to quote him at some length.

What is our mental image of a decision maker? Is he a brooding man on horseback who suddenly rouses himself from thought and issues an order to a subordinate? Is he a happy-go-lucky fellow, a coin poised on his thumbnail, ready to risk his action on the toss? Is he an alert, gray-haired businessman, sitting at the board of directors' table with his associates, caught at the moment of saying 'aye' or 'nay'? Is he a bespectacled gentleman, bent over a docket of papers, his pen hovering over the line marked (X)?

All of these images [continues Simon] have a significant point in common. In them, the decision maker is a man at the moment of choice, ready to plant his foot on one or another of the routes that lead from the crossroads. All the images falsify decision by focusing on its final moment. All of them ignore the whole lengthy, complex process of alerting, exploring, and analyzing that final moment.[8]

Perhaps Simon is a little bit scathing about the horseman, the coin spinner, the grey-haired board director; perhaps he is too severe about the moment when the decision-maker may say 'Let's go!' It may be, also, as will be discussed later in this chapter, that his own description of the build-up process in decision-making is too structured. But his central emphasis is that there *is* a process and that it is misleading to concentrate attention on the final moment when, as it were, the button on the camera is pressed and the snapshot taken. That is convincing and the examples Simon gives are thoroughly persuasive. He writes of the adoption of large electronic computers by many companies to deal with their accounting and other data-processing work and points out that although computers had become commercially available in the early 1950s few companies had investigated their use in any detail before 1955. Consequently he says 'For most companies the use of computers required no decision before that time *because it hadn't been placed on the agenda*'[9] (italics added).

Computers first came into extensive use in industries requiring 'complex computations for engineering design', and it was after that that businesses with a large number-processing load – insurance companies, accounting departments in large firms, banks – discovered these new devices and began seriously to consider their introduction. From this stage, the activity which led to the preparation of programmes for payroll preparation went forward and 'Few companies having carried their investigations of computers to the point where they had definite plans for their use, failed to install them.' Simon's delineation of the elements in decision-making may be summarized as

intelligence ⟶ finding occasions for making a decision, e.g. becoming aware of the possibilities of computers;

design ⟶ finding possible courses of action, e.g. developing the first computer programmes for payrolls;

choice ⟶ selecting one among a number of possible courses of activity, e.g. deciding to install a computer.

First implications for management

Everybody would be likely to agree that a proper understanding of the nature of decisions and decision-making will be useful in a general way because it is always beneficial to clear the ground of misconceptions. But what are the practical implications for management of the broad reasoning so far?

The first practical consideration is that decisions depend on an information input but that the information will not be complete, will not be perfectly accurate, and will not be all in one place at one time: it will be incomplete, imperfect, and dispersed. The result is that managers will typically be making decisions on the basis of information that would be fuller (though not necessarily better) if only they waited another day, or week, or month. This is inevitable because information takes time to collect and arrive sequentially – in sequence, day by day. Thus, a critical point in the management process is *when* to decide, and a practical problem is whether the organization has mechanisms for obliging managers to make up their minds. Of course it is not a purely bureaucratic matter: it is partly a matter of the quality of the individuals and their ability to decide. Or again, there are many instances in which there are well-established rules and clear statements about what information is required. For example, the criteria for recruitment of managers, or for their promotion from one level of management to a higher one, may be quite specific. The setting of deadlines is an important part of the decision-making machinery.

The problem is more difficult, however, when the information is ambiguous and open to differing interpretations or when the decision is not routine. In the first instance it may be a matter of comparing the performance of two individuals in different business functions or of evaluating performance of a non-measurable kind. The second may be a major decision about a new departure in the business or a new factory building in a fresh location or a substantial reorganization. Experience suggests that the need for a decision has to be brought to a head and that this requires a machinery of decision-making. If information is incomplete, what means exist – formal or informal, committees or luncheon meetings – to settle on when the cost in time, effort, and money of continuing to assemble data is outweighed by the delay in decision-making which will result?

The same factor applies to the imperfect character of information. There is an oft-quoted saw uttered by the American film comedian Will Rogers, that 'It's not so much what folks don't know, as what they do know that ain't so' that constitutes the problem. In other words, it is the fact that what managers, like other people, believe to be information and fact may be inaccurate. One important reason for this is that many of the things that are regarded as facts are really hypotheses, i.e. suppositions and theories. A company may observe a fall in its sales and state it as a known fact. The decision as to what to do about it will depend on some proposition about why sales have fallen, e.g. the level of its product prices, decline in customer attention. This proposition is not a fact: it is a hypothesis, testable no doubt, but of a different status from the information that sales have fallen. Hence management quite often depends on having adequate means of evaluating and reviewing the information on which decisions have been based, particularly when it is appreciated that the information of today may not be valid for tomorrow.

This means, in other words, that part of the decision-making process is the persistent up-dating of information; it is not something which is 'given' on a fixed, immutable basis but, rather, something requiring persistent monitoring and review. The same applies to the assumptions which underlie the decision processes. If these are in-valid, the course of action chosen is hardly likely to be correct. (See Chapter 7 below for an extended discussion of these points.)

There is, then, the point about the dispersed nature of information. It is sometimes assumed that the data required for decisions are available to managers in one place, spread out on the table for them to look at, and then to decide. But of course information may very well be compartmentalized: some with the accountants, some with the marketing people, some with the research and development de-partment, and so on. One of the problems in the making of decisions can lie in this compartmentalization, particularly if the professional experience and pride of separate groups become added complications.

This is a very important point to which a number of writers have given considerable attention. Different parts of an organization, as Simon points out, may act as its 'sensory organs', in other words, its means of securing and analysing information. Market research, for example, is one way of securing information on which a business may base its sales plans. Specialist personnel may be appointed for the sake of the expert knowledge and skills they possess and for their ability, therefore, either to make decisions or to provide the kind of information which enables other people to do so. Would it not be simple, asks Simon, to match information with decision, so that the individual who knew would also decide? 'The basic difficulty in this', however, 'is that not all the information relevant to a particular decis-ion is possessed by a single individual.'[10] Decision-making in a manage-ment context has features peculiar to organizations precisely because information within them tends to be fragmented and dispersed.

This argument involves a number of points which have a great practical bearing on management. An individual who decides, as an individual, to buy a bar of chocolate or a motor car may have to search for information – availabilities, prices, and so on. In an organization, what has to be known for any decision is dispersed to different individuals and departments, and it has to be brought to-gether through the creation of a machinery of communication. Thus effective systems of communication must underlie the decisional role of management. Moreover, with the best will in the world, in-formation will often not flow, as is required for effective decision-making, because it is not asked for. It is not too difficult to imagine the following exchange. 'Why didn't you tell me?' 'Because you didn't ask' or 'And how should I know that you needed such information?' or 'How should I know that such information exists?' Here again, therefore, there arises the need for management machinery, formal or informal, not only to generate information but to ensure that *relevant* information is assembled at the decision points.

This first practical consideration has stemmed from the proposition that the information at the disposal of decision-makers is incomplete, imperfect, and dispersed. The consequence for management and for students of management is the recognition that one of the critical tasks of managers is the creation of decision-making machinery and periodic review of its effectiveness. Professor Loasby, an economist who has very much concerned himself with decision-making, has emphasized that, just as the production facilities of a business govern what it produces and the efficiency with which it produces it, so the machinery of decision-making governs the decisions which are made and the efficiency with which they are made. The procedures and processes are the 'fixed capital' of decision-making.[11]

This argument clearly applies in the context of the incomplete and imperfect quality of information, but it is no less important in respect of its dispersal. There is probably no formal machinery which will fully meet the requirement, and there is therefore a strong case for an informal network. Some of this can, oddly enough, be provided for, and might be called planned or built-in serendipity. A university, with its tradition of discussion in the common room, is perhaps the prime example, but a civil servant, employed in a firmly-structured organization, remarked that in one post he had found that 'A surprising number of ideas (around fifty per cent) start life informally, e.g. from social conversation or irrelevant reading.'[12]

These points lead naturally to the second practical consideration in decision-making: how do matters come on to the agenda for decision? Herbert Simon, as was noted above, wrote of the introduction of computers, that it did not require a decision in the early 1950s because it had not arrived on the agenda. Another Nobel Laureate in Economics, Kenneth Arrow, makes the comment that 'it is a commonplace of everyday observation and of studies of organization that the difficulty of arranging that a potential decision variable be recognized as such may be much greater than that of choosing a value for it.'[13]

The point that Arrow is here emphasizing is that the difficult problem in any organization in the making of decisions is to ensure that the responsible people in the organization (the managers in a business enterprise) should be drawn to consider what the relevant considerations are. What can managers do to ensure that items come up for decision? Simon speaks of what he calls 'evoking mechanisms' and 'attention directing processes': an example he gives relates to the adoption of innovations. He stresses the apparently simple point that things are done when people can be induced to attend to them and says that this is borne out by studies of the introduction of innovations.[14]

In the simplest terms, this means that part of the decision-making process involves creating mechanisms which will induce managers to think about the 'right' things. These mechanisms may be of many kinds, again formal and informal: committees, working parties, project groups, external contact with universities and colleges. It was the custom of the Midlands Postal Board at one time, for example, for members to lunch together after the monthly board meetings and use the occasion to discuss wide-ranging topics in a fairly unstructured way. It was also the chairman's custom to invite an outside visitor to the lunch, such as the director of the Chamber of Commerce, and discussion with him formed part of the learning process by which the board might inform itself on matters of current and future interest in its markets and potential markets. The very structure of the board at that time – a core of full-time executives and a number of part-time non-executive members from industrial and academic life – was meant to provide a means for widening the agenda considered by the business. Although these may seem trivial examples, they were in fact quite important in helping the board to see where points of decision might be arising in the future. They represented a modest but valuable attempt to scan the environment *actively*, even if in some instances they revealed only 'a cloud no bigger than a man's hand.'

The upshot of these first implications of the general analysis of decision-making is the recognition of the importance of *information*. Indeed, it could be said that the *decisional* role of managers, which is widely accepted as a central – perhaps *the* central – characteristic of the management task, consists of translating information as input into commitments to courses of action which are outputs. These commitments are expressed in the decisions by which the courses of action are chosen and resources allocated to them. It is not too much to say that the products which are made by firms are human knowledge and information turned into physical objects and services. The decision by a business to manufacture and market a product represents managerial assessment of information and of possible opportunities. The trick, as Sir Adrian Cadbury expressed it, is to turn a possibility into a profitable venture.

Because, however, information is not given to managers like tablets of stone on which all they need to know is immediately to hand, management is not a simple activity. Information has to be looked for, and evaluated, and decisions have to be made as to how much information is needed: there can be such a thing as information overload, i.e. more information than can be handled, so that the decision-makers find their task obscured by the volume of (irrelevant) data.

On categories of decision

There are different kinds of decisions, and different levels or layers of management carry responsibility for the various decisions. It is possible to classify decisions in a number of ways, some of which are now set out.

Perhaps the simplest thing to note is that decisions differ in size in the following sense: some affect more people, more money, more output than others. Another aspect of size is the number of business functions which are affected: in some cases only one specific activity or one department of a business may be involved; in others a number of departments may be influenced by the decision; in still others the whole company may be concerned. It would be more accurate, in fact, to classify decisions in this respect by what may be termed degree of complexity.

Figure 1 expresses, in simplified form, some different ways of looking at decisions and draws attention to a distinction between programmed and non-programmed, a distinction which appears frequently in the management literature. Consider a series of possible cases. A fire brigade is required to respond to an alarm with a series of responses which are habitual, according to what is properly described as a drill. The decisions which are relevant to these responses have already been made and are expressed in the strict routines which have been established. There may be routine procedures, less dramatic in consequences than a fire service, but equally standardized, in the conduct of a business in matters both small and large. These may be concerned with procedures for issuing items from stock, authorizing payment of expenses, approving projects over and above a certain level. In all these instances, the task is to administer the rules and observe the procedures; the administrators who were quoted as saying that they administered the ordinances saw themselves as following a strictly defined set of regulations.

FIGURE ONE

A CLASSIFICATION OF DECISIONS

Characteristics / Classification	
1. SIZE	Numbers involved: people. Expenditure: amounts of money, investment. Output, sales.
2. COMPLEXITY	Number of departments affected or concerned. Number of products, geographical areas.
3. PROGRAMMED	Established rules and procedures: appropriate to well-structured problems. Can often use quantitative techniques.
4. NON-PROGRAMMED	Ill-structured problems: no established rules. New problems.
5. STRATEGIC	Concerned with the product-market pattern of the firm: what it supplies and the markets it serves.
6. ADMINISTRATIVE	Organization structure: the way the organization is built – its departments, divisions, etc.
7. OPERATING	The continuing operations: prices, inventory, production scheduling, etc.

The important points about programmed decisions are that management has already worked out the set of rules, and it is possible to go on applying them because the problems for which they have been designed are repetitive. How to handle each problem does not, therefore, require fresh rules, although there may still be the task of deciding whether a particular case falls within the rules. But this is only one end of a scale at the other end of which are to be found the non-programmed decisions, those for which there are no rules exactly prescribed in advance. If a company is considering extending its operations into a country in which it has never previously been involved, or diversifying its product line by engaging in the manufacture of products which it has never before handled, what exact rules can it adopt to make its ultimate decisions? In some instances, of course, it can analyse very carefully and estimate very sophisticatedly a number of the possible consequences. For example, in looking at mechanization of letter offices, the Post Office in Britain made rigorous efforts to estimate likely cash flows on various assumptions, and the estimates were carefully considered. But there were many imponderables, and there must have been points in the decision process at which top management had to make judgements of a 'one-off' character. There must be, in other words, a kind of 'intuitive' jump from the analysis and the measurements to the eventual decision. This is all the more so because some of the information is ambiguous.

This continuum, as Simon calls it, of programmed to non-programmed decisions is simply a convenient way of looking at the different tasks of decision-makers. As he says, it is a grey continuum in which the words programmed and non-programmed are the black and the white. The distinction between the two is important for managers in the decision-making process because it raises quite different issues as to how to equip managers to cope.

It can readily be seen that the separate categories of decision outlined in Figure 1 can, in fact, be expressed in a condensed classification, as in Figure 2 (overleaf).

This classification is neither exhaustive nor wholly rigorous, but it serves to emphasize that the strategic decisions which determine where the business is going – its product and market directions – do not lend

FIGURE TWO
SIMPLIFIED CATEGORIES OF DECISION

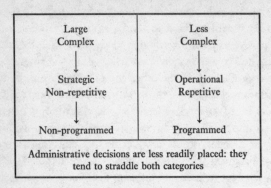

Large Complex	Less Complex
↓	↓
Strategic Non-repetitive	Operational Repetitive
↓	↓
Non-programmed	Programmed

Administrative decisions are less readily placed: they tend to straddle both categories

themselves to programmed decision-making and to the management techniques, often quantitative, which are appropriate in other areas.

To sum up this section: it is possible to consider decision-making according to 'the *degree of programming*: the extent to which the procedure for reaching a decision is prescribed.' Within any organization, business enterprise or non-business, procedures will have been built up over a period of time: the organization will have 'learned' how to set out certain kinds of decision, what rules to apply. The machinery of the business, its committees, departments, units, will be, at one and the same time, the channels along which these decisions flow and the instruments by means of which they are effected. In most enterprises, it is only too easy to concentrate on those decisions at the expense of strategic decisions which involve innovative thinking and departures from accustomed routine.

Some comments on the ways in which decisions are made

Writers on decision-making in management stress how much remains to be studied about how decisions are actually made. If this were only a matter of research for the intellectual satisfaction of scholars, it would be interesting, but perhaps not particularly important for managers. Knowing *how* is, in fact, of practical use because it may throw light on what is required of aspiring managers and may help towards improving management methods.

One critical aspect is the need to avoid stereotypes. For example, in this chapter, emphasis has been placed on a process by which information as input is transmuted into decisions as output. This is a perfectly reasonable way of looking at the decision process. But it is not a universal explanation of how decisions are made. The decision-maker has sometimes been imagined as saying 'I decide, then I justify . . . Now that I have made my choice, I need to find good reasons for it.' This may seem a cynical comment but it is not necessarily so. To begin with, managers have an upbringing and ideas in their organizational experience which are not always in the forefront of the decisions they make, but which nevertheless influence or predispose them to move towards certain decisions. This 'feel' may be very important, based as it is on judgement built up through accumulated experience: in Cadbury Schweppes, for example, there was a 'feel' about the geographical balance of the business and this had an effect in the decision to expand into North America. A similar approach has been mentioned by the senior executives of Tarmac, the big construction company. From a practical point of view, it is important that this accumulated experience be pooled and utilized: it should certainly not be dismissed as mere rationalization after the event.

So much has been written about risk and uncertainty in decision-making, so much about the unknowability of the future, that it may seem that life for managers is at worst an impossibility, at best a nightmare. Yet in fact managers do make decisions which have objective consequences; firms do successfully market new products, and managers lead interesting and rewarding lives. Does this mean that there is an unbridgeable gap between the stringent propositions of the theorist and the real world of the managers?

The first part of the answer to the question is that not all the world is all that obscure all the time: or to put it another way, managers, like other people, behave as if there were some systematic stability in the world. A great deal of the activity of managers must consist in doing what they have done before – only more so, or maybe less so. To that extent, quite a number of the decisions which have to be made are likely to be modest adjustments at the margin. There is no need to assume that the bottom is going to fall out of the market every day or that customers are going to behave with dreadful irrationality. Of course, managers may be wrong and the bottom *may* fall out of the market – once is enough! A large order *may* be lost, a major client *may* transfer his custom elsewhere. Thus, managers need, in principle, to be alert to possible instabilities in the system, especially in a turbulent environment of changing technology, competition, legislation. But over a significant proportion of their work, they have to assume that life has its regularities.

The second element in the answer is that there is a variety of decision-making responses which depends on many factors: the personal qualities and training of the decision-makers, the size of the enterprise, the kind of market environment in which it is encapsulated. Sir Isaac Wolfson has already been quoted on management ulcers: on a similar occasion, the same question was put to a chairman of I.C.I.: 'Does it worry you to be at the head of so large a business?' The reply was, basically, that small-scale businessmen worry about their small-scale businesses and large-scale about large-scale activities. Words like leadership and charisma can, it is true, be 'escape' explanations: nevertheless, decisions are made because there are men and women capable of making them in circumstances which call for them to be made.

One of the most important points to recognize is that it is not organizations which make decisions. To say that a firm entered a fresh market, or that a university instituted a new degree programme, does not mean that the organization decided – as if it were a single being. This, as will be seen later, means that members of the organization made decisions of such a kind that the result was an entry into a market, the establishment of a new degree. They did so, of course, as part of an organizational system: that imposes constraints, but it also provides support in skills, information, and the ability to decompose decision-making into separate parts which can utilize the varieties of expertise and experience.

Reference has been made to the work of Witte. This was carried out over a number of years by the Institut für Entscheidungs- und Organisationsforschung (Research Institute for Decision and Organization) of the University of Munich. A detailed examination was made of 233 decisions to purchase electronic data-processing sytems by German organizations which had not previously had one. The research took the following hypothesis: consider a decision-making process which is complex and innovative, and which involves numbers of persons. Then the final decision will be more efficient if the following processes are pursued:

- recognition of the problem
- collecting information
- developing alternatives
- evaluating alternatives
- choice.

In other words, this is a picture of decision-making in successive phases. But Witte's conclusions (and remember that his is only one of numbers of studies of decision-making) do not show that the decisions were typically made in *the orderly sequence*, nor, in the four out of 233 instances in which they were so made, were they more efficient. Witte remarks that

> We believe that human beings cannot gather information without in some way simultaneously developing alternatives. They cannot avoid evaluating these alternatives immediately, and in doing so they are forced to a decision. This is a package of operations, and the succession of these packages over time constitutes the total decision-making process.[15]

This difficult example has been chosen here because it illustrates not only the variety of processes and stages, but also the complex nature of decision-making with its large numbers of sub-decisions. In the above quotation, there is also an implicit indication of how managers cope with the complexity: in the decision-making process there is a continuing set of overlapping operations, and these involve numbers of people who contribute to the total package. It could be said, also, that this underlines the importance for management of creating an environment and mechanisms of co-ordination which are helpful in what may be a complex – and in that sense untidy – set of operations.

If the world of decision-making does not conform to the orderly models and if the reasons for this are embedded in the nature of the management situation, is there no help to be found in the prescriptions for executive behaviour which are to be found in so many texts? There are two kinds of answer to this sceptical question. One answer is to admit that decision-making requires of managers certain kinds of sensitivity and flexibility which lie outside the neat stages of the models: there is also a 'political' dimension to decision-making in organizations and more ambiguity and uncertainty than analysis may allow for. A second answer, and one which is not in fact incompatible with the first, is that the idea of an orderly sequence from, say, problem recognition to choice may have value as a standard and as a discipline, and as a means of focusing management attention on critical themes.

CHAPTER FOUR

STEP-BY-STEP IN DECISION-MAKING

The management of organizations is a practical activity: incrementalism has been developed as one explanation of how it is done. It deals with the way in which decisions are made by managers in business enterprises and public administration and suggests that the process is one of step-by-step. Managers, according to this view, do not usually proceed by means of a grand plan with clear, predetermined objectives: they do not consider *all* the possible courses of action and then choose the 'best'. They work in a more limited, practical and pragmatic way which takes into account the lack of knowledge and the uncertainty about the future which all human beings must experience. They have to take into account, also, that inside an organization, business or non-business, decisions may involve many people and departments. Effective action depends on the ability to bring together the different interests and objectives of these separate individuals and units.

The origins of 'incrementalism'

'Incrementalism' appeared on the scene as a major idea in the work of Professor Charles E. Lindblom in the United States. He set it out in 1959 in a paper entitled 'The Science of "Muddling Through"' and elaborated it in a number of his subsequent books and papers.[1] He applied 'muddling through', which he also called 'disjointed incrementalism', to the making of decisions in public administration, and he was clearly thinking within the framework of the democratic constitution of the United States. His approach could, however, be applied, with some modifications, to management in business, and Lindblom says this quite explicitly.

What is the idea, and how does Lindblom explain it? Fundamentally he contrasts two modes of decision-making. The first he calls the *comprehensive* or *root* approach: the other, which he calls the *branch* method, is his 'muddling through'. In the first case, the maker of decisions is able to look at the complete picture:

- he has a clear objective: he knows exactly what he is aiming at and what his objective means;
- he knows all the alternative methods open to him and he knows the outcomes of all those methods.

In these conditions to 'choose' the best is nothing but a reflex action: the world is just like an automatic telephone exchange. The caller knows what number he wants and how to dial it, and the number is automatically obtained.

In a later paper entitled 'Strategies for Decision-Making', Lindblom expressed this ideal model in a detailed if slightly less extreme form by quoting Theodore Sorenson's picture of decision-making: [2]

first: agreement on the facts;
second: agreement on the overall policy objective;
third: a precise definition of the problem;
fourth: a canvassing of all possible solutions . . . ;
fifth: a list of all possible consequences that would flow from each solution;
sixth: a recommendation and a final choice of one alternative;
seventh: the communication of that selection; and
eighth: provision for its execution. [3]

Such a comprehensive picture of the making of decisions is considered by Lindblom to be much too simple: in fact, he uses the phrase 'simple minded inadequacy' to describe this ideal. In its place, he substitutes the *branch* method: policies are adopted step by step, i.e. incrementally; decision-makers will restrict themselves to policies *not too far different* from existing policies and 'must make do with dodges and stratagems that are not scientifically respectable.'

The practical consequences of this idea are discussed in detail below: first, however, what are the differences in approach to which it gives rise? The Sorenson model and other models like it specify a completely consistent, rational construction of strategy, and they make the following assumptions:

1. That in principle there is no difficulty in agreeing on the facts. But what is a fact? A business may experience a fall in its sales, and all its executives may agree on the sales figures: once, however, they try to give the reasons, it is not at all obvious that they will agree. Is the fall due to a price change, or to a change in the weather, or to competition from a new product . . . ? What are the 'facts'?

2. That an overall policy objective is meaningful.
Of course in one sense that is true. Business enterprises, governments, clubs, have general values and purposes: for example, a company may wish to make profit, or grow; a government in framing its taxation may do so in terms of its attitude towards enterprise. When it comes down to brass tacks, however, in every organization there will be more than one objective and it will be necessary to strike a balance in practical situations. Some objectives may have to give way to others or be only partly attained, or be reformulated in the light of experience and differing interests.

The same kind of reasoning can be applied to the third proposition, which involves the assumption

3. That there is a precise definition of the problem (on which everyone can agree).
Again, in one sense that is true: everyone may choose which problem to regard as *the* problem, but there may also be real differences of opinion. Suppose, as Lindblom himself puts it, there is an increase in the number of violent crimes. Some people will say that the 'real' problem is a decline in public morality or in religious belief; others will say that it is the inadequate number of policemen. Cause and effect are inextricably intertwined.

Even if there were no difficulties in these three propositions, the idea that it is feasible to consider all possible consequences of all possible alternatives is clearly untrue. Lindblom takes the point further when he talks about the 'cost of a decision' and says:

In buying a house, for example, which is a relatively simple decision problem, would we propose to spend $100,000 to canvass and list all possibilities and all consequences in choosing among a variety of houses in the $20,000 price category? [4]

Moreover, buyers in this instance would have a good notion of the likely costs of the decision, but whether it proves to have been worth it will only be discovered after the event. As Lindblom says, 'although the costs of making a decision can often be estimated with reasonable accuracy, the payoff typically cannot.'

Thus, to take another example, it may be possible to make a reasonably accurate estimate of the cost of developing a new manufacturing plant (although this is by no means straightforward and certain), but it will typically be more difficult to assess whether the expenditure will turn out to be as worthwhile as hoped for. Decisions have to be made in the context of an uncertain picture of the likely payoff from a course of action.

Incrementalism and the business enterprise

Lindblom was certainly thinking in terms of the public sector and specifically of government and government departments. Professor James B. Quinn, however, in his book *Strategies for Change: Logical Incrementalism* and elsewhere, was dealing with American business enterprises. His theme was that 'Instead of following rigidly prescribed formal planning practices . . . managers in major enterprises . . . *consciously* . . . move forward *incrementally*.' [5]

Quinn approaches the problem of strategic decision-making in major business corporations in much the same way as Lindblom looks at public administration. Just as Lindblom puts up the Sorenson picture and then severely criticizes it, so does Quinn set out the textbook picture of the formal, rational planning process. He lists twelve features as the main elements, which may be summarized as follows:

1. Analyse internal strengths and weaknesses of the company.
2. Project profits, sales, etc. of current product lines.
3. Analyse external environment for opportunities and threats.

4. Establish broad goals for parts of the group.
5. Identify gaps between expected and desired results.
6. Communicate plans to divisions.
7. Generate specific plans from divisions.
8. Occasionally make special studies of alternatives.
9. Review divisional plans and sum these for corporate needs.
10. Develop long-term budgets.
11. Assign implementation of plans to specific groups.
12. Monitor and evaluate performance against plans and budgets.

Anybody who has read an introductory textbook on principles of management or more advanced textbooks on strategic management and business policy will recognize these elements. And generally some process of this kind is *prescribed* as the desirable way to formulate and implement corporate strategy. Of course it is well-understood that managers do not always behave in this way, but the assumption is that their failure to do so is a defect which could be remedied if they knew better, if they were better trained, if they had better (more) information, if the organizational structure were improved, if a greater use were made of management techniques. Even uncertainty is invoked rather like the quotation which Gimpl and Dakin reproduce:

A long range weather forecast should be obtained before leaving, as weather conditions are extremely unpredictable. [They go on to say] Try to avoid falling into the trap of believing that because you have a weather forecast you can control the weather.[6]

Forecasts are valuable but they are not guarantees, however precisely they may be stated.

Quinn's argument is that managers do not and *should not* make their strategic decisions in the way set out above. He suggests four ways in which effective strategies are really made, which in summary are:

1. In any business enterprise the system consisted of a number of sub-systems with different people, different information needs and so on. Each sub-system looked at company-wide issues in a disciplined way but did so incrementally and opportunistically.

2. Each sub-system had its own requirements in timing and other considerations.

3. Because each sub-system had its own limits on its knowledge and had other limits also, and hence tended to act incrementally, the total enterprise behaved in the same way, because the company as a whole had to deal with the interactions between the strategies of the sub-systems.

4. Skilful managers who use this step-by-step approach are not 'muddling through'. They are deliberately using this as a management approach to improve the quality of strategic decision-making and purposive action.

The different sub-systems – units, groups, departments – are all parts of the company as a whole, but each one of them is viewing its own problems and those of the company from its particular perspective. Each one will have its own strategy or sub-strategy, made in step-by-step fashion, while the company has to take into account the interconnections between the individual strategies. Throughout a whole enterprise, therefore, processes of discussion, consultation, explanation and negotiation will take place.

First reflections on incrementalism

The idea that the formulation of strategy in business enterprises is a process of 'muddling through', however skilful, may seem both startling and difficult, and Quinn's four points need a lot of explaining. This section spells out the idea in greater detail.

There are two things which incrementalism does *not* mean. First of all, it does not mean that managers should never use analysis or quantitative methods or behavioural sciences. Second, it does not imply that 'muddling through' means being in a muddle. Lindblom says in fact that he had perhaps made a mistake in using the phrase and especially in referring to *disjointed* incrementalism. In doing so, he may have given the impression that administrators and managers work by intuition – that they do not go in for systematic analysis – that running an organization is just a matter of 'politics'. This was not his intention. Nor, though he is critical of the 'rational' models of decision-making, does he argue that men behave *ir*rationally: he is not saying that policies and strategies are formulated simply on how the decision-makers happen to feel that day.[7] Professor Quinn is quite clear in saying that '. . . the formal planning approach is excellent for some purposes', but, he continues, 'it tends to focus unduly on measurable quantitative forces and to underemphasize the vital qualitative, organizational, and power-behavioral factors that so often determine strategic success in one situation versus another.'[8]

Although Lindblom's work is not identical in approach with that of Quinn, the implications of both, or some at least of those implications, are much the same. What may be termed the 'management science' approach to strategic decision-making in organizations tends to place a heavy reliance on theory, a generous dependence on the availability and quality of information, and on quantitative techniques and measurement. Formal planning systems assume that the objective of the enterprise can be specified uniquely and *unambiguously*, in advance, and that the whole process can be rigorously systematized. Built into this picture, it is true, are warnings against inflexibility, but it is often regarded *as part of the planning process* that flexibility should be provided for.

The essence of incrementalism in the business enterprise, as envisaged by Quinn, is contained in his words 'vital qualitative, organizational, and power-behavioral factors', and in his emphasis on the processes through which strategic changes are brought about. He is careful to speak of *logical* incrementalism: the processes are neither haphazard nor accidental.

By definition, an established business does not start from 'square one'. It has an existing body of assets in the form of plant and equipment, marketing channels and goodwill, organizational structure, knowledge and managerial skills. Knowledge and expertise will have been built up over a prolonged period: existing strategies will have been instituted and the associated organizational adjustments made at a cost. The current behaviour of the firm has involved a process of learning about what it wishes to do and how it does it. But this is not the end of the matter, since any business is engaged in an ongoing activity. Part of that continuing activity is designed to carry out the operational plans and everyday tasks which arise from existing strategies: part of it is to pick up problems and opportunities from which new strategies will be generated.

This means that strategy is not a once-for-all blinding flash of sudden vision: it is neither reposed in one individual nor located in one room in the organization. Of course there is an important element of creativity in strategy: that is what entrepreneurship is about. Professor Shackle characterizes it as the business of creating the future. But the present is not an island to itself; it has a history and an accumulated learning which influence current decisions. Thus strategy may grow out of concerns and pressures which have been building up over a considerable period in which, for example, the company has come to feel that its geographical balance or its product range is not quite right. Ideas may arise in any part of the organization, and pieces of the strategic change will be put into place before the strategy is completely worked out.

There is another aspect to be considered as a result of this picture of an ongoing process in business behaviour. Strategy is not made in an instant: it is, as Ansoff has remarked, a costly and time-consuming activity.[9] A business cannot simply accomplish its tasks if top and senior management issue instructions and then behave as if that meant that the job was now done and the strategy firmly and finally instituted. The formulation of strategy requires a complex process of initiating, discussion and debate, persuasion and agreement: it is only with a bird's-eye view or with hindsight that an organization appears to move as if it were one man. Quinn's logical incrementalism is conceived as a management process in which managers deliberately engage in the activity of securing consensus and commitment.

In the section which follows, some practical consequences and examples are given but at this point it should be noted that the step-by-step approach suggests that because of the built-up capital in physical assets, manpower, and expertise, consensus and commitment will be more readily secured if new developments are *not too remote* from existing strategies. In this way it will be easier to carry managers with change because it will lie within a framework which is reasonably familiar to them and which makes use of their training and knowledge. Incrementalism also takes into account that within an organization there will be a multiplicity of goals – not just one – and that 'No human being – except an essentially insane person or one in dire circumstances – can consistently pursue only one goal.' That quotation from Professor Quinn follows his comment that 'organizations satisfice because they are made up of human beings.'

Some practical consequences of incrementalism

So far in this chapter, the idea of incrementalism has been considered in general terms and without any serious distinction between Lindblom's ideas, primarily designed for public administration, and those of Quinn in the context of the business corporation. This section is largely concerned with business, although some attention is paid to the public sector.

To the extent that incrementalism induces an organization to confine its steps in policy and strategy to areas with which it is experientially familiar, two consequences are likely to follow. A company will be disposed to stick to its last. Thus, for example, Sir Adrian Cadbury defined the business of Cadbury Schweppes in terms of its channels of distribution such as supermarkets. Although in fact he also defined it in terms of snack foods, he argued that there was nothing really incongruous in also selling Jeyes Fluid (a disinfectant), since this was also distributed through supermarkets.[10] On the other hand, he eschewed such businesses as restaurants because these lay outside the competence of the company as measured by its accumulated experience and expertise. He thought, also, that a company could only consider a very limited number of options at any one time: the ultimate decision was, moreover, itself an outcome of decisions previously made.

This brief and simple example illustrates a number of the features of incrementalism: limitation of the scope of change, restriction of the number of options considered and hence explicit neglect of other possibilities and other possible outcomes. Furthermore, in this company as in a number of others, considerable emphasis was placed on the need to *carry* management with strategic change, to secure that understanding, consensus and commitment which Lindblom and Quinn both underline.

A further feature is the illusory nature of the 'best' decision. In another context, Quinn quotes one chief executive as saying that 'the future can make fools of us all.' He was referring specifically to the undesirability of hoisting one's flag too dramatically to large objectives, explicitly stated in advance, which in the event might prove impossible to achieve. This is not only a matter, however, of caution in avoiding possible loss of face: it also arises because an enterprise (i.e. its executives) has to learn, from experience, which of the objectives are feasible and which not, and how to balance and trade off various objectives one against another. In addition, time is a critical factor in decision-making, and the recognition that decisions cannot wait indefinitely: there has to be a point at which the available information is 'enough'. Sir Anthony H. M. Bowlby, at that time head of Guest, Keen & Nettlefold Screw Division, commented that for this reason decisions were characteristically made with incomplete data – otherwise somebody else would get there first. A second-best decision taken in time is preferable to a better one taken too late.[11]

These references to decisions themselves being the outcome of other decisions and to the importance of time clearly show that the making of decisions is a complex process through time. Among the examples cited by Professor Quinn are those in which it is emphasized that it is not always easy to say when 'the' decision was taken. Major changes in a business enterprise may be spread over a number of years. The managing director of a trading company in the fast-moving entrepreneurial society of Hong Kong described major strategic change in his company as a process in the course of which it was transformed from its traditional activity of general 'middleman' between Western business and the East into a company specializing in knowledge of particular industries. It could thus offer particular expertise and trading links. The changed strategy and the accompanying effects on the internal structure of the company – for example, the recruitment of graduates was a departure in company policy – had come about in response to changes in the speed of communications which had altered market conditions for trading firms. But the time span from management's early perception of the moving environment to the point where it could be said that a new strategic disposition had been fully adopted was ten years. This is perhaps a particularly long time, but it does not imply that it took ten years to introduce the strategy: it means that the process of perception, analysis, discussion, introduction of pieces of the strategy at different times, was going on over that period.[12]

In public administration and other characteristically non-business environments, a similar argument can be pursued. Lindblom suggests a university example:

a university committee is asked to advise on reorganization of the curriculum. No one is wholly clear about just what a college education is supposed to accomplish, nor does he have unlimited time to give to the question. Nor has anyone on the committee enough time to canvass exhaustively all the possible curricula that might be designed. And obviously no one can possibly predict the consequences of one curriculum as distinct from another. Although all these things will be thought about and although the committee members will be prepared to exercise their judgement in coming to some kind of a conclusion, the three prescriptions – clarify objectives, canvass all possibilities, and investigate the consequences of each possibility – call for investigations that could easily occupy the committee's energies for several years and even so would not be completed.[13]

If this appears to be a somewhat exaggerated picture, it should be remembered how, in practice, a course of action can be agreed upon in the face of differing possibilities. Boundaries have to be drawn, some paths deliberately excluded, a reasonable number of options considered. In this way, complex problems can be rendered more manageable and decision-makers can more readily accommodate themselves to the reality of uncertainty.

Incrementalism, formal planning, and corporate strategy

The examples given in the preceding section can be matched by many others, and they are part of the debate which has surfaced in recent years about the usefulness of formal planning systems and grand designs of corporate strategy. Some of this debate is discussed elsewhere in this book: in this section, consideration is given primarily to the connection with incrementalism.

Writers like Lindblom and Quinn do not argue that it is pointless to think in terms of the strategic direction of an organization, nor do they say that formal analysis and planning are a complete waste of time. Minkes and Nuttall, in their study of five major British companies, build on the idea of incrementalism in the formulation of strategy but in doing so they also give attention to evidences of the part played by planning thought and corporate philosophy.[14] Quinn thinks of formal planning as a means of improving data and communications, making managers more receptive to new ideas, providing measures of performance, obliging managers to look at the central ideas that unify the various activities with which they and their companies are concerned.

Some management thinkers are less sympathetic to planning approaches and to the emphasis on the concept of corporate strategy, of which they say that 'as theoreticians elaborated . . . and taught it to generations of students, it became a more sterile way to view a business.'[15] However that may be, most of these thinkers say one or other of the following things:

- formal planning may or may not help, but it does not describe the process by which strategy really takes place.
- the formulation of strategy involves numbers of people at different levels in the organization.
- an excessive emphasis on techniques, formal planning, and on the concept of corporate strategy is inimical to the things which really matter . . . such as entrepreneurship, and the ability to deal with 'ambiguity, uncertainty, and interdependence in organizations'.

Incrementalism is thus one stream in an important flow of ideas about the reality of the management process. It focuses attention on careful study of how strategy is made from inception to implementation. Of course there are questions which are left unanswered: for example, how does a step-by-step explanation allow for dramatic change, and how does it take into account the dynamic contribution of the entrepreneurial individual in the organization? These and other questions are considered in the discussion of strategy and planning.

CHAPTER FIVE

ARE DECISION-MAKERS REALLY RATIONAL?

The problem of knowledge and information dominates much of management life: it clouds it with uncertainty but at the same time creates the need for management. Managers have to make decisions precisely because information is imperfect; if they had perfect knowledge, they would have no problems of choice and hence no decisions to make. Since, in reality, it is necessary to assemble and to evaluate information, managers require organizational means, formal and informal, by which they can carry out these tasks. The collection and assessment of data take time so that a crucial management decision is: *when to decide*. Practitioners of management are always having to come to terms with the limitations on their knowledge and to find ways of arriving at decisions and courses of action within that framework. Can they, in these circumstances, still be described as acting rationally, and if so, what kind of rationality do they possess? This raises the idea which has become known as bounded rationality.

First steps towards limited rationality

The name of Herbert Simon has come up repeatedly, because his work was of seminal importance in the study of decision-making by executives. Curiously enough, it is not referred to nowadays quite as much as might have been expected, partly because of subsequent work but partly, perhaps, because it has become a kind of common currency. At the very least, however, Simon's ideas constitute the groundwork for an examination of administration and management in a world of limited knowledge.

In his book *Administrative Behavior*, Simon set out to consider what he called administrative man and to try to establish the basis of a theory of organization and administration.[1] Economic man, he said, the man who is put up by the economists, is impossibly omniscient. He knows exactly what he wants; all the alternatives available to him are known; and all the possible outcomes of all the alternatives are also known. Of course economists know very well that human beings do *not* have complete knowledge and that they cannot perform all the computations which would be necessary to evaluate all the possibilities which might, in principle, arise. Moreover, economists have tried to grapple with the problems of uncertainty and of information flows. For all this, readers who have studied or who are studying economic theory will be familiar with its characteristic methodology: consumers who have entirely consistent preferences, demand curves which are known, costs and prices which are given, and so on.

Economic performance is fundamental in the management of enterprises, whether it be interpreted in terms of business effectiveness and efficiency open to market test, or of non-market organizations which are trying to assess the utilization of their resources by other means. Hence it is not unreasonable to make a critique of the economists. But Simon also points to the other end of the scale, where, he considers, social psychology had been too ready to emphasize the absence of rationality. The 'past generation of behavioral scientists has been busy, following Freud, showing that people aren't nearly as rational as they thought themselves to be.'[2] Neither the rationality which consists in saying that individuals consistently seek to maximize (and know how to do so) nor the irrationality which rests on arguments of the kind that 'the pressures of a social group can persuade a man he sees spots that aren't there' appeals to Simon. The behaviour of people in organizations is not, it is true, completely or globally rational, but it is nevertheless intendedly so. It could even be described, as some writers have done, as non-rational or quasi-rational, by which those writers are emphasizing that the members of organizations are oriented towards tasks and do try to achieve purposes. This, again, is not irrationality: it is rational in kind.[3]

In other words, people in organizations are aiming at goals, seeking to accomplish tasks, and do at times succeed: in that way, they are doing their best to be rational. But because of the limits of human knowledge and computational powers, their rationality is limited. It is a *bounded rationality*: that is the kind of rationality which human beings actually have; and it should be noted that it stems from the inevitably imperfect character of human knowledge, the unknowability of the future, and from 'the impossibility of making full use even of present knowledge'. Consequently, argues Simon, the decision-maker cannot choose the best possible solution to the problem: he does not know it because he does not know all the possible solutions. And even supposing that there is a collection of solutions to be known, it could be very costly to go on searching.

What, therefore, does the decision-maker do? According to Simon, instead of maximizing (much as he would like to), he *satisfices*. The introduction of the notion of *satisficing behaviour*, a compound of 'satisfactory' and 'sufficing', was a most important step. It contrasted with economic man who is a maximizer seeking the best solution, somebody whom Simon called 'his cousin ... administrative man', who settles for solutions which are good enough. This is satisficing behaviour of which 'adequate profit' or a 'fair price' are illustrative criteria.[4]

Two examples will illustrate the point in a general way. There is the comment that a person does not look for the sharpest needle in a haystack but stops when he has found one sharp enough to sew with. The other concerns the man who comes to a town as a stranger and wants to get a haircut. If he were working to the model of perfect rationality, he would know exactly what kind of haircut he wanted, would know all the barbers available and their capacity to satisfy his wishes, and all their prices: he would thus be drawn inevitably to the optimal choice. In reality, the man will go to a barber: if he is not satisfied, he will go next time to another barber, and go on until he gets a haircut which meets his level of aspiration, a level which *satisfies* him. It is true that he could go on looking – but it would be at a cost which he can estimate for an additional benefit which is unknown.[5]

These examples, and Simon's reference to such things as 'adequate profit', have a useful bearing on management. To begin with, they draw attention to the point that decision-makers (and managers have a decisional role) have to *search* for solutions: they are not faced with a given batch of solutions out of which they pick the best. Secondly, they have to decide when to stop looking, and, according to Simon, they do so when they have 'a needle sharp enough to sew with'. Thirdly, and this is perhaps particularly important, since decision-makers cannot consider all possibilities, they will deliberately limit the number and type they consider. They will look at only a *segment* of the world: they are content with a simplified picture of the world rather than attempting to deal with it in its complex and confusing totality.

It has already been suggested in the previous chapter that administrators and executives, faced with the problems of dealing with a complex world, simplify their tasks by limiting the number of possibilities they are prepared to consider. Simon points out that the decisions which have been made in the past narrow down the range of choice available in the present. Strategies are what he calls 'time-binding', by which he means that when a person or an organization has embarked on one strategy, it creates a commitment which it seems better to go on with than to abandon entirely. Thus, when an individual has settled on one trade or profession or a business has settled on one product line, they have by that choice already circumscribed the number and type of options which they are obliged to study. A shoe manufacturer, as Simon puts it, 'does not need to reconsider every day . . . whether it should be in the automobile business instead.' This does not mean, of course, that the individual or organization will never change, but it does mean that they do not need *continuously* to review what they are doing. Adrian Cadbury made a similar point when he observed that it was not feasible to try to evaluate one option against all the other available options. But it is this very limitation of options, at any one time, which enables decision-makers to act rationally, because it confines the segment of the world and the volume of information they have to consider to what they can handle.[6]

This argument applies at the levels of both individual and organization. An individual who has trained for a highly specialized academic discipline, for example, has by virtue of the previous decisions narrowed down the present choices. Cadbury Schweppes, having defined themselves as a supplier of snack foods through such channels of distribution as supermarkets, have held that restaurants are outside their decision range. Similarly, Newey & Eyre (the electrical wholesaler subsidiary of Thomas Tilling, prior to the acquisition of the latter by another company) excluded from its purview diversification outside electrical goods.

Thus, the nature of the decision range which results from past choices or which is imposed by positive decisions of the kind 'we define our business as . . .' and 'we stick to our last . . .' is precisely the kind of limitation which permits rational behaviour because it makes the world more manageable. There is a whole volume of information in the world to which decision-makers need pay no attention because their decisions and their results will not be affected by it. This makes it the task of individuals and executives alike to settle on the information which matters and to discount what does not. The example of the shoe manufacturer is straightforward, but there will be many other instances that are not. The general principle which Simon states, that the executive in the real world makes sense out of it by not trying to take absolutely everything into account, is valid. But it is an important aspect of management that managers have to *decide* where to set the limits and to be prepared, as Simon indicates, to review the limits from time to time.

Limited rationality and satisficing behaviour further considered

It is not part of the present purpose to make a detailed examination of the different meanings which have been ascribed to the idea of rationality nor to make an exhaustive criticism of Simon's ideas. It is only fair to say, however, that they have been criticized on various grounds. For example, are there not many decisions in which much, perhaps most, of the information required is in fact available? Are there not many optimizing techniques and does not satisficing simply mean that decision-makers optimize within the limits of their information (i.e. 'imperfect' optimizing)? And is it really true that in searching for solutions decision-makers stop *as soon as* they have found one which is good enough?

These are important questions and the fact that they are only lightly touched upon here is not to underrate them. But since the emphasis is on management, and since Simon's ideas are being used as a launching-pad, the implications for understanding business and organizational behaviour are the relevant considerations. There are also many other writers who have, in their different ways, attempted to explain management behaviour in the context of a real world of limited knowledge, and satisficing behaviour is perhaps to be regarded as only one possible mode among numbers of others, by which individuals and executives in organizations arrive at their courses of action. The idea of bounded rationality with the attendant emphasis on the need to search for information, to limit alternatives and to consider only a segment of the world retains a special significance.

Looking back at the analysis so far, this significance can be observed in a number of contexts. One which has been noted above is the tendency of enterprises to limit their agenda by defining their businesses within certain parameters. Some writers have gone so far as to put this into quite limited confines: Teece, for example, discusses the 'evolutionary theory' of the firm in this way:

The firm ... is conceived as having a distinctive package of economic capabilities of relatively narrow scope. The information required for the functioning of the enterprise is stored in routines, in which much of the underlying knowledge is tacit, not consciously known or articulatable by anyone in particular. As Nelson and Winter point out: 'Routines are the skills of an Organization.'[7]

A further implication which is drawn from this comment is that the history of a firm is important, since what it is and what it can do depend on what has been established through time. This applies, not only to its accumulated physical assets, but also to its knowledge and skills, its rules and conventions. Thus it can be said that the managers of a business have a built-in body of experience which influences performance. There is a legacy of people and of experience, as Cadbury called it, which does not set the firm in a permanent mould, for ever and ever, but which governs its possibilities at any time and for some time.

Without ascribing to Simon either explicit or implicit parentage of particular theories or examples, a family link can be noticed with his views on looking at only a segment of the world and his reference to the shoe manufacturer who does not have to think about the automobile business. When the (top) managers of business enterprises set boundaries to the scope of activities which they regard as appropriate to their *competence*, as measured by physical assets, organizational capacity, knowledge and expertise, they are not demonstrating an irrational neglect of opportunities. They are meeting, as was noted above, 'a necessary, though not sufficient, condition of rationality'. But this raises serious questions for management of how to respond to a changing environment; how, for example, to move outside a range which changing circumstances may have rendered inadequate.

Consider some current problems in the management of universities in Britain. Looking at their history and routines, it can be seen that they were largely designed for undergraduate and postgraduate degree courses and for research. In recent years, partly as a result of new ideas and partly under the pressure of financial difficulties, universities have engaged in a variety of post-experience courses (typically, short courses for practising managers and professional workers) and in other activities such as the setting up of industrial parks. It has required a considerable shift in thinking, and has occasioned considerable problems of organization, to move from traditional fields and to exploit opportunities for which the existing assets and personnel were not initially designed. These departures from the traditional pattern have also required adaptations and innovations in the administrative methods of universities. Nevertheless, in this instance, the extension of the agenda still leaves it within a range of topics and requirements which is not too unfamiliar. The process is still incremental, even if the increment is quite large.

But now consider a somewhat different example. In his book *Management Cases*, Drucker gives the case of a businessman who had built up a chain of supermarkets, garden centres, home-service centres, and greeting-card stores. He then turned to consider outdoor wear and restaurants and found his managers sharply divided: one group opposed the idea of 'fashion', the other equally opposed 'personal service' and the catering business. Drucker makes his businessman pose to his managers the question: what is our business? [8] In other words, he puts the management question: what can come on to our agenda with the reasonable assurance that we shall be competent to manage it? But while there is a great deal of evidence to suggest that management does limit its range of decisions, it is clear also that the boundary of a firm's competence is a shifting one and that part of the task of management is persistently to evaluate where it lies and where it can be moved.

One significance of the idea of bounded rationality in this particular context seems to be that management is obliged to make decisions about what it should be doing. There are choices to be made because managers cannot have an all-seeing eye and enterprises need management devices to scan the environment, to search for information, and to detect or seek out opportunities, precisely because knowledge is not a 'given'. Lindblom remarks that 'we need decision-making strategies for making the most of rationality', that is to say, good management strategies which simplify the complex problems with which organizations are sometimes faced and help managers to be rational. They are better able to match their methods to their tasks because they are prepared to leave some things out of account. At the same time, this creates the problem of managing for change (without waiting for crisis or disaster to provoke it).

Rules and routines

So far, the analysis has been mainly concerned with the larger issue of strategic choice as this is affected by uncertainty and complexity. There is also the question of how to manage other issues: this is partly reflected in Simon's reference to 'adequate profit' and similar guidelines, partly in the rules and regulations which are used in organizations to manage their affairs.

Every organization has its rules and regulations, its 'standard operating procedures'. For managers, they perform three general functions. First of all, rules are a method of control: for example, the issuing of parts from inventory may be governed by the need for a permit, the payment of cheques by the requirement for countersignature by a senior member of the organization. Simple rules of this kind provide a means of forward control and of checking back. But, secondly, rules are a means of reducing uncertainty, since the members of an organization are provided with a systematic way of doing things and can safely assume that other members will follow the same procedures. Thirdly, the routinization of decision-making by the establishment of rules and procedures is a means of economizing management time, although, of course, some time will be expended in deciding how far a particular rule applies in any particular case.

More generally, Sir Geoffrey Vickers remarks that

Whether the conditions of control exist or not, human behaviour, whether in business or out of it, is basically rule-governed. It is guided by applying to the situation, as perceived, rules which take one or two forms. They may take the form – 'To achieve this, do that' or 'To avoid this, do that'. Alternatively, they may take the more general form 'In these circumstances, do this'; or 'In these circumstances avoid doing that'. Since whatever we do has far more effects than we intend or can foresee, we act on rules of the second more general pattern more often and more justifiably than we realize.[9]

This wider comment by Vickers illustrates the point that rules are a means of encompassing uncertainty, even in very uncertain situations. They will range from the very strict to the more elastic – in the sense of being open to interpretation – and they may be informal as well as formal. Since, moreover, decision-makers do not possess complete 'given' knowledge, they have to try to learn from experience. The rules and regulations of their organizations may be taken to represent that accumulated experience, a kind of sunk capital of procedures. Where they are formal, they may be of the kind 'Keep inventory at such-and-such a level', 'Replace stock at predetermined levels', 'Give discounts above a certain size order from a customer'. Where they are informal, they may be of the kind 'Use your judgement as to giving a discount' (within certain limits) or, as in the case of the managing director of a large company mentioned above, 'Do not drop in on branch managers without asking them first.' Since rules are partly designed to let people know where they stand, those self-imposed rules, hallowed by experience, are also real parts of the procedures and 'way of life' of the organization.

There is another, though related, sense in which rules and standard procedures arise from, and help managers to deal with, uncertainty, which again may be exemplified in the case of non-profit organizations. The question is very often asked in universities, social service institutions, schools, or hospitals: what criteria can be adopted for judging the allocation of resources between departments? Faced with what appear to be intractable difficulties, it is nonetheless essential that some guidelines, that is, rules of behaviour, be adopted. In practice, the managers or administrators do not arrive at the 'best' criterion or set of criteria. They devise criteria which appear to work and which are broadly accepted by the participants in the process: in a university, the staff-student ratio is a typical example of such a criterion and is used as one indicator by which departmental requirements for academic staff may be assessed. The point is that the problem is dealt with, not by looking for the best possible method but by recognizing that there is a problem to be dealt with and that standard procedures can be devised for the purpose. These procedures may be the subject of debate and disagreement, but they work as long as people can go along with them.

While this example is from the non-profit sector, it is not unique to it. There are departments of business enterprise – personnel is a notable case in point – which may be described as secluded from an immediate single test of, say, return on capital or earnings per share, and which have to be evaluated by other indicators. It is perfectly obvious that some indicators are thought to be better than others: a common reply to those who criticize a particular indicator (on general grounds or because they think it gives their department an unfair deal) is 'Can you come up with a better one?' But to say that people prefer what they call 'better' to what they call 'worse' is not the same thing as saying that they arrive at decisions by the use of optimizing models.

A number of writers, notably Simon, Cyert and March, have given a good deal of emphasis to the part which is played by standard practices and set procedures in an organization. As was noted above, they provide stability and a means of reducing uncertainty, because they give individuals established rules on how jobs are to be done. This means, also, that individuals do not have to relearn each time what they should do in a particular case.[10]

If it were perfectly obvious what should be done in each and every situation, managers would not have much to do, or, at all events, they would not be required to show initiative or to exercise judgement. In a sense, rules and procedures say to the decision-maker: 'You don't have to think about it, just follow standard practice.' Even where rules are not so precise, there will often be the accumulated force of precedent, the experience which managers have had and which forms part of what the organization has learned through time. But there will be occasions when the manager has to consider:

- what rule applies in this case?

or

- does the rule which normally applies in cases of this type apply in this particular case?

or

- should the precedent be ignored in this instance?

Thus, standard procedures, rules and regulations help in the process of management and set a framework of expectations within which managers are enabled to categorize problems and to make decisions in the light of an established system and an acquired experience. Where, however, the situation changes is precisely where decisions are required for which there are no rules because the organization has not previously encountered them in that form. The problem of facing up to technological change and innovative investment is a classic example of this type of problem in a rapidly changing external environment. Rules can tell managers *how* to do things: they cannot be expected to tell managers *what* things they should be doing. The incremental adjustments discussed in the previous chapter constitute one explanation, in fact, of the way managers may adapt so as to reduce the pressures of uncertainty.

The question of objectives

One topic which must be touched on, albeit in a preliminary way at this stage, is that of objectives. There are two major aspects which are important from the point of view of management:

1. Managers work in organizations: hence, the decisions which concern them and in which they are involved are made in organiza-

tions. (see Chapter 7 below). To understand how management functions requires understanding of the nature of organizations, and of the way they work.

2. Organizations consist of individuals, units, and departments, in other words, persons and groups. Individuals have more than one objective in life: to earn a good salary, to secure promotion, to make a happy marriage, and so on. This may be put even more emphatically with respect to organizations. Each level of management, for example, may have objectives specific to it and each department of an enterprise will have its objectives and will see problems from its perspective. Sales, finance, research and development will all have legitimate objectives. Sales managers and sales representatives want a product which it is good to sell, backed perhaps by strong advertising; research managers will argue for withholding some funds from current activities to provide for research into future products and processes.

The very existence of multiple goals means that there is something called goal conflict. It should not be inferred from this that there is a state of war, only that there is not perfect compatibility among the objectives; it is not possible to satisfy all of them completely all the time. Consequently, it is one of the tasks of management to manage conflict, to enable the organization to function, not by pretending that differences do not exist, but by resolving conflict to an extent that makes possible the continued and successful life of the organization. In the circumstances of real management life in which there are different interpretations of information and different assessments of priorities, successful management cannot imply perfect agreement among all members of an organization. It is successful because it succeeds, despite disagreement, in being able to arrive at agreed courses of action. Here again, the exposition of the views of Lindblom and Quinn, particularly the latter in his analysis of the *political* process by which strategic change is generated and implemented in business enterprises, demonstrated one approach to the understanding of management.

It might be asked, very understandably, is this not an unduly complicated approach to the study of management and the tasks of managers? Is it not, from beginning to end, a matter of profit: is it not 'the bottom line' that counts? If managers keep in front of them the objective of profit maximization, and if business is entre-preneurially directed by the search for (the most) profitable op-portunities, will not the whole business be expressible and manageable in relatively simple terms? Speaking as chairman of Tarmac, R. G. Martin, an industrialist who was fully alert to the idea of multiple objectives, also specified the acid test as (maximizing) earnings per share. And if business is operating in a competitive environment, will it not follow that firms whose managers do better in profitability will outstrip those who pay it insufficient attention?

These are difficult and complicated questions and there is more than one way of attempting to answer them. It is not really a question of whether profit and profitability are important in a business enterprise: they clearly are. But it is a question of asking how far profit explains the business decisions which directors and managers make. Profit, as a number of writers have said, can certainly be interpreted as a constraint on the individual business in the sense that the requirement of being profitable delimits and limits the options which can be selected. Profit is also, as Drucker puts it, the test of the validity of decisions. But it is quite another matter to relate this to motivation, since even if decision-makers were personally un-interested in profits, they would still have to make them. This would be true, says Drucker, even for archangels, and he observes 'That Jim Smith is in business to make a profit concerns only him and The Recording Angel. It does not tell us what Jim does and how he performs.' [11] This is very like an observation made by Adrian Cadbury when he was talking about consensus in decision-making. He said that profit was a consequence of achieving objectives, and that to say that decisions had been made to meet a particular target did not adequately explain 'why some things were in and other things were out.'

Drucker's argument is that 'there is only one valid definition of business purpose: *to create a customer*', and that to this end the mana-gers must establish and work to a set of objectives in the separate functions of the enterprise. The main point, however, in the context of management activity, is contained in the phrase '. . . does not tell us what Jim does . . .' To say to managers: 'Go ahead and make a profit', or, more stringently, 'Go ahead and maximize profit' will not explain what it is that managers have to do as part of their management task, however useful it may have been in developing economic theory to assume that firms are profit maximizers.

Whatever view is taken of Drucker's detailed argument, and of others who write in a similar vein, it does seem quite clear that the *process* of management cannot be adequately explained in terms of a single, unambiguous objective for the whole enterprise. To begin with, if Simon's strictures on maximization are taken into account and if *some form of satisficing* is widespread in the sense of target rates of return or market shares, for example, the question arises: how do managers arrive at such targets? If, moreover, it is accepted that there are multiple objectives, which cannot be added together, how does management arrive at agreed courses of action? In another context, Loasby uses the trenchant phrase: 'one can often optimise a model; one can never optimise a situation.' And management is situational: managers are in situations and are part of a network of relationships with other managers.

The preceding analysis in no way minimizes the significance of profit as an engine of enterprise. Nor does it rule out the use of profit as a standard of performance, as, for example, in profit centres within a business. It is only to emphasize what has already been said, that what managers actually do and how they perform cannot be explained by saying that firms do or should maximize profit. Nor can management be developed and managers trained by issuing a single prescription, whether the maximand be profit or something else.

Is rationality dead?

The argument of this chapter has partly been a half-way summing-up, and this calls for a tailpiece. Since so much emphasis has been placed on imperfect knowledge and uncertainty, the tailpiece is addressed to the question: what is left of rationality in the process of management? The answer is: a very great deal. Managers are both rational, in the sense that they purposively relate the tasks they perform and the methods they employ to purposes they wish to achieve, and reasonable in that the 'political' processes in which they are engaged are consciously designed to maintain the organization through seeking to reach agreement.

But the rationality which must be ascribed to managers and administrators is *bounded* by the limitations of human knowledge and human computational capacities. Lindblom's thesis is a good way of expressing the importance of this for big problems: his schema might be represented as:

● try to raise the level of rationality in decisions

● recognize that when problems become too big, they have to be simplified (bounded rationality)

● in other words, accept a simplification which results in some 'loss' of rationality

● recognize that there is a balance between this loss and the irrationalities of problems which are too complex for the mind

● develop strategies for decision-making so as to make the most of rationality.

None of this is meant to imply that managers should not use the modern management techniques which have come powerfully to their aid in recent decades, particularly in the ongoing operations of business in which they can contribute so greatly to efficiency. Nor does it suggest that managers must live in a fog of imperfect knowledge: on the contrary, it is the existence of uncertainty and the need to make judgements whose outcome cannot be absolutely foreseen, which gives rise to the need for managers and to the challenges that the business of management presents to them.

CHAPTER SIX

THE INNOVATIVE MANAGER

The preface to a recent collection of readings on innovation includes the following passage:

> The management of a stream of innovations is extremely complex. A large percentage of all new products fail, many successful and innovative small firms do not make the transition to more mature larger organizations, and many large firms (or business units) become bureaucratized, stifling their ability to innovate. There is, then, an important temporal dimension to be understood: (1) why is it that some firms are more innovative than others at a point in time; and (2) why is it that some firms are able to be innovative over a period of time (or over the product life cycle) while other firms have severe difficulties in being innovative after initial success.[1]

Professor Handy was quoted earlier on the need for managers to be able to live in two time dimensions, the present and the future; Professor Drucker stresses the entrepreneurial role of the manager. These statements mean that a requirement is imposed on managers to be innovative, in products, markets and organizational form. This chapter is devoted, therefore, to the idea of innovation, and since innovation is brought about by people and requires to be managed, the chapter is concerned with the manager as innovator. The implication of this is that innovation does not stop at invention: it embraces the whole process by means of which new technologies and products are brought to commercial fruition (or, in non-market situations, are introduced into the product stream).

This is an extremely wide topic and one on which there is a growing body of literature. It raises somewhat different problems from those with which the managerial framework is normally equipped to cope.

As Professor Gold has pointed out, it would be superficial and mis-leading to treat the managerial task in respect of innovation, research and development as nothing more than a special case of, say, the analysis of investment decisions. For, as he says, the 'distinctive problems' for management which innovation generates begin just where the decisions it requires 'differ from the purchasing, produc-tion, marketing and other problems which the prevailing decision-making framework evolved to handle.' They involve 'an array of targets'.[2]

Uncertainty has been emphasized already in earlier chapters: in-novation is uncertainty itself, for the products and processes have to be developed, future costs are typically unknown, production and marketing problems may be as yet indefinable. Thus, many questions are wrapped up in the single topic of innovation.

- how are ideas generated in an organization?
- what is the appropriate relationship between scientists, engineers and managers?
- what are their different motivations?
- what part is played by organizational innovation?

The study of innovation and of its management involves a variety of disciplines and business functions: economics, organization theory, psychology, marketing, and so on. It is also part of the process of strategic change, because innovation introduces new products and methods and changes in corporate structure. The topic is, therefore, part of an interrelated set of topics which embraces organization, strategy, and corporate planning. Moreover, innovation can be looked at as a question of how organizations learn, how the managers within them come to make changes and to adapt to them.

This is a demanding matter for managers, since innovation is what J. E. S. Parker has called 'management intensive.' Innovation, whether it be in new products and processes or in the forms of organization adopted by an enterprise, is disturbing and costly. If a company has chosen to put a great deal into its research and development effort, to be an innovative enterprise, it has drawn on itself at least two managerial consequences. In the first place, it will have to give managerial time to the introduction of its new activities and to the learning processes which may be associated with change. In the second place, the management of the research function requires considerable skill, for, as Parker says, 'Creative personnel cannot just be left to follow their research hunches.'[3] Success also depends on how the innovative process is managed, how projects are selected, and how the research effort is fitted into the general requirements of the business.

Thus, what can be said for R & D applies also to the demands made on managerial time and talent, by the need to understand the organizational consequences of innovation and to make the organizational changes which may be required.

There is another element in the innovative process which a number of writers have stressed, most recently Foxall in his book *Corporate Innovation*, and that is the interrelationship between seller and purchaser. This can be a potent force in generating innovation; Foxall writes that 'innovation is not only a managerial activity but a facet also of customer behaviour.'[4]

On the importance of innovation

Everybody agrees that innovation is important. Drucker regards it as one of the two basic functions of a business, the other being the related function of marketing. Rosemary Stewart thinks of it as increasingly significant for many companies. Foxall refers to innovation as something which is sometimes inherently valued for itself, for the novelty and stimulus of change, but essentially as the means by which living standards are enhanced and men and women can enjoy products and services hitherto unknown to them. As he points out, however, the term is very difficult to define. At a seminar at Birmingham University, Isaac Wolfson was asked about innovation in Great Universal Stores, of which he was chairman. He recounted this anecdote. He had noticed that in many miners' homes in South Wales there was nowhere in the passage where coats could be hung. The company subsequently sold large numbers of small fixtures which met the purpose and were suitable for the narrow space available. Is that, Wolfson asked the seminar, what you would call innovation? Why not indeed? It was certainly managerial alertness to a market opportunity, even though the instance is of modest dimensions. An accumulation of modest changes may form a continuum through which an enterprise moves and develops its innovative character.

From the point of view of management, there is much to be said for Professor Kanter's extremely broad definition, which sees innovation as the whole series of stages by which new ideas, products, and processes are brought into being. The improved transmission of information within an organization, better methods of costing or of project evaluation, different ways of arranging production methods, would all be examples – some quite modest, some substantial – of innovation as thus defined. Invention is only a first stage: the implementation of innovation requires further stages through which management brings ideas to commercial fruition. One consequence of this admittedly very wide definition is that it emphasizes that there is more than one source of innovation within an enterprise. The entrepreneurial spark which is one facet of management may be struck in more than one part of the organization and may include 'creative use as well as original invention.' [5] John Neville and Adrian Cadbury both thought that the trick was to bring ideas from all parts of the corporation and to turn them into marketable products. Hewlett-Packard, the American high-technology electronics company, prided itself on what it called Management by Wandering Around as a means of encouraging initiative and an 'open-door policy' in the organization.

In this context, the Wolfson example is clearly innovation. So are improved methods of storing data, whether they be computer-based or, for example, the transfer of library cataloguing from cards to microfilm. The establishment of a new department or faculty in a university falls under the heading of innovation, as does the computerization of student records. There is, in other words, a great variety of innovations, ranging from small to large, from more or less continuous to more dramatic breaks in technology, products, and organization. Consider some of the larger changes in Britain in the course of thirty or forty years. The gas industry has been transformed from the coal-based manufacture of gas and coke to the supply of natural gas from the North Sea. Railways, which once accounted for the direct consumption of many million tons of coal per annum for steam engines, now consume coal only indirectly, through electricity supply based on coal. Looked at over the relatively long period of, say, seventy-five years, the retail trade has witnessed the rise of packaged products and convenience foods. Organizationally, it has seen the development of department stores and supermarkets.

The importance of innovation from the standpoint of its effects on the flow of goods and services hardly needs to be underlined. Looked at in terms of the individual enterprise, 'the innovative objective', in Drucker's opinion, 'is the objective through which a company makes operational its definition of "what our business should be".' Interestingly enough, he holds that

Deliberate emphasis on innovation may be needed most where technological changes are least spectacular. No one in a pharmaceutical company or in a company making synthetic organic chemicals needs to be told that survival depends on the ability to replace three-quarters of the company's products by entirely new ones every ten years. But how many people in an insurance company realise that the company's growth – perhaps even its survival – depends on the development of new forms of insurance, the modification of existing policies, and the constant search for new, better, and cheaper ways of selling policies and settling claims? [6]

It might be argued that Drucker writes in something of a missionary style, that he may underestimate the ability of firms to rub along for a surprisingly long time in apparent defiance of a changing world. In the past, for example, it was certainly the case that a snapshot picture of the firms in an industry would have shown a very wide spread in technological levels. Salter illustrated this in respect of a number of industries in Britain, with consequent substantial variations in productivity between best-practice and other manufacturing plants. [7] But it remains basically the case that innovation is a critical, perhaps *the* critical, factor which determines the continuing position of an enterprise in the market place.

There are several implications for management. The first stems from the proposition that innovation is management intensive: it takes up a considerable amount of time and effort both in learning about change and in persuading others to accept and adapt to it. The second is that there is often a close link between innovation in products or processes and organizational change. The example of the British gas industry is instructive in this regard, since the change in source of supply altered the relationship between the central body of the industry (at that time known as the Gas Council) and the divisions (based on regions), in effect strengthening the centre. This can be explained, to a great extent, by the fact that the divisions had now become part of a system of distribution instead of being areas of production. In its turn, organizational innovation may facilitate the introduction of new products, because it may make it easier to handle diversified product lines.

A third consequence for management is that the process of innovation itself has to be managed and that, as pointed out above, it has special characteristics which differentiate it from the 'conventional' areas of production and marketing. This is particularly true in those enterprises where research and development departments play an important part in the structure. The rise of the industrial research laboratory is, in fact, one of the striking phenomena in the history of the modern business corporation in this century, and with it, there are two further, related management consequences. One is

... a higher proportion of managers and specialists. The management ratio, that is, the proportion of management staff including specialists, to total employees, varies greatly between companies of the same size. Part of this difference is due to the number of staff employed in research and development.[8]

Rosemary Stewart, from whom that passage is quoted, goes on to refer to a study of employment structure in fifty American companies since the Second World War which demonstrated that the proportion of senior staff increased most in firms which were making the most changes, and increased hardly at all in firms which were innovating least. The other consequence is that managers have found themselves managing 'the knowledge workers' in a world where more employees are professional and technical people.

On the sources of innovation in an enterprise

A great deal of what has been written about innovation has dealt with it at the macro-economic level; very frequently, it has been concerned with technological change and with the kind of transformation which has brought wholly new products and processes on to the market. This approach has also emphasized the rapidly increasing rate of change, the consequent shortening of the product life cycle, and the problem of product obsolescence which this entails. In the face of all the uncertainties and unpredictabilities of innovation, economies now dispose of technologies and products which were barely imagined even a short time ago. Progress from the quill pen to the word processor has changed the physical production of the written word; the ubiquitous ballpoint pen has thoroughly changed the position of the 'fountain pen'. What began as a market stall has been transformed into Marks and Spencer; the paradigm of the grocer is no longer the corner store, it is Sainsbury's in Britain, Krogers or National in the United States.

The transition in that paragraph from the economy as a whole to individual instances and particular firms is a deliberate elision. All the changes, large or small, have to be explained at the micro-economic level: their conception, development, and implementation took place, generally, within firms and required decisions by managers. Of course this was not always the case: sometimes governments were involved, sometimes joint ventures involving more than one firm. But essentially the argument holds good that innovation, which from a macro-economic point of view looks like a broad economic stream, is in fact made up of the innovative activities of business enterprises and other organizations. More precisely, it is the outcome of innovative decisions by their members. Foxall expresses the relationship between the macro- and micro-levels in this way:

... macro-economic prescriptions for innovation-led economic growth have tended to ignore those facets of new product development which are bound up with the strategic and market-oriented competences which determine the performance and effectiveness of companies. Theoretical assumptions which relate innovation and growth, like prescriptions for state intervention in the innovative process, are generally based upon a definition of innovation which casts it as invariably discontinuous. But innovation is a process which includes continuous as well as discontinuous product development. Effective innovation occurs, moreover, as a function of corporate managements' perceptions of and responses to their strategic needs for innovation.[9]

The question then is, as Foxall himself stresses, what generates the process of innovation, how is it stimulated, and how is implementation made effective?

It is extremely difficult to postulate a comprehensive explanation of what dictates the flow of innovations: indeed the evidence is that many tributaries contribute their shares to that river. There is a certain mythology, to which Burns and Stalker have drawn attention, in which 'the boy Watt ... dreaming in front of a boiling kettle ... later invented the steam engine', although in reality other factors, among them Watt's friendship with Joseph Black, who discovered latent heat, and his personal acquaintanceship with the industrialist Roebuck played a significant part in his technological work.[10] The lonely captain on the bridge is not in fact isolated: he is part of an extensive and complex network with back-up from other people. Note that this is not to undervalue the significance of the individual of genius or talent, nor to deny the crucial function of the individual at the top. It is only to say that to be at the top is not to be entirely alone, because the individual is also a member of an organization; nor is the organization devoid of a history.

To say that there is a structure in the managerial adoption of innovations may be only to detect a pattern after the event: that pattern is real, but at the time that managers are making the decisions, they may not see, or, at all events, they cannot foresee for certain, what the pattern will be. It is useful, therefore, to look at some of the specific ways in which innovations may come about, without for the moment distinguishing carefully between small and large changes, strategically-planned or tactically-responding.

- Minkes and Foxall cite the instance of a paint manufacturer who introduced an anti-condensation paint which would be effective at high altitudes: the initial impulse came from an airline which was seeking a remedy for problems with condensation.
- while that may be regarded as a relatively small case, the same authors also refer to extensive research which demonstrates that 'need input' from customers is tremendously important in generating innovation by producers.[11]

These points reflect the role of the product user in stimulating suppliers to innovate, and it is clear, therefore, that one of the major tasks of management in the supplying units is to maintain contact with the users, to be market-oriented. The research studies referred to above were in such areas as chemical products, equipment innovations, and scientific instrument innovation, where customer pressure might perhaps be expected. But similar characteristics are to be encountered in the marketing of final consumer products.

● this leads to another element in the generation of new product opportunities: this stems, not from the R & D departments of firms, but from consumer-oriented identification of product opportunities, such as 'gap analysis, segmentation analysis, comparative market analysis, group (consumer) discussion and brainstorming'.[12]

These points underline the extent to which innovation is related to the capacity of management to detect and manage the firm's market relationships – not simply to manage its research and development function. Drucker's emphasis on the identification of the market as the primary management task (in the entrepreneurial sense of management) is in the same mode of thinking.[13]

There is no need, however, to make too sharp a distinction between these approaches, particularly where major innovations are concerned. This is admirably brought out by Christopher Freeman in a number of comments which can be expressed in three points he regards as fundamental:

(i)   Scientific research stimulates new discoveries and technical possibilities

Firms which can monitor these advances can be the first to take advantage of them, and strong R & D may help them to turn these possibilities into competitive advantage

(ii)   Firms which are in close contact with customer requirements can spot potential markets

and may thus convert new ideas into new products and processes . . . of course, this does not guarantee that they will succeed. They may be outstripped by competitors 'or by an unexpected twist of events whether in the technology or in the market.'

(iii) 'The test of successful entrepreneurship and good management is the capacity to link together these technical and market possibilities, by combining the two flows of information.' [14]

Freeman's succinct analysis of the technical and market relationship is wholly apposite to innovation as an idea in the context of management. The reference to a link is part of the conception of innovation as 'a coupling process'. Imagination is the antecedent spur; the imaginative mind is where the process first is found. In the continuously changing, fluctuating relationship where science and technology, discovery and development, organization and market, eventually meet, an idea becomes a marketable product.

Ideas, particularly in the major innovations with which Freeman is concerned, are related to something termed 'creativity', which, fortunately, does not have to be closely defined here. Innovation – remember that this involves bringing ideas to (commercial) fruition – requires a management process to create and manage the climate in which new ideas can be communicated and to manage the stages through which they become part of the product and process repertoire of the business. Successful innovation depends critically on the quality of entrepreneurial management and on the firm's communications, both internally and with its customers.

But which managers are primarily responsible for managing the innovative process in business enterprises? A simple answer would be to say that managers at all levels should be concerned, particularly in the light of the very broad definition of innovation given by Professor Kanter and others. Looking at the question in the round, it can be said that effective innovation, particularly in the case of major innovations, depends on the commitment of top management. Why is this so?

First of all, major innovation is a strategic matter, particularly in capital goods (new kinds of plant and equipment), but also in big changes in product line in consumer goods. Strategy is a matter which must concern the top commanders of an enterprise. Secondly, top managers are in the strongest position to secure the resources required for big changes: the innovator, in Freeman's words, 'must have enough knowledge of the way the firm works to know *how* to get things done.' In the example cited earlier of a relatively modest product development, the paint firm in question was quite small, and its top executives (in this case they were brothers) would have dealt directly with the matter as well as with larger ones. In the large and complex modern business corporation, the position of the innovative managers in the hierarchy acquires a special significance.

Clearly, however, there is no reason why the requirement should be restricted to the top levels. Innovation, it has been pointed out, is related to the customer, so that marketing, sales, market research, sales representatives are, so to speak, the firm's antennae for communication with the external environment. Sometimes the relationship may be very direct and specific, as in the case of the paint manufacturer cited above or as in another instance, where the sales representatives of a printing ink manufacturer were the channel through which printing firms were able to transmit their requirements, which might be new and specialized. Sometimes it is expressed in a strong commitment to the function of market research – not only marketing existing products in existing markets, but also actively scanning the environment for new possibilities. In discussing this type of scanning of the world beyond the boundaries of the business, it is possible to see how greatly innovation comes to depend on the ability of managers to spot the significant factors and then to carry through the consequential changes.

This may apply in somewhat unexpected areas. For example, in the

University of Birmingham, some twenty years ago, a member of the Department of Political Science, Henry Maddick, was instrumental in setting up as a separate unit a Department and Institute of Local Government Studies. This was primarily designed to provide short courses for local government officers and to develop research in local government affairs. The bulk of this activity was financed outside the traditional mechanism of the University Grants Committee, by course fees and research grants and contracts. The Institute included development administration in its work (courses in local government for Third World countries, in fact, preceded its British courses). All this was a significant innovation in university work; it had academic roots in Maddick's interests in local government as an area of study but it also came about, it may be understood, because Maddick had detected a fresh 'market' which required a different approach to the organization and finance of courses of study.

The establishment in the early 1970s of the Health Services Management Centre in the same university is another example. It stemmed from the proposition that the university study of management, often seen as very much a matter for business, could be fruitfully extended to hospital administration, in courses for administrators and graduate entrants, and to research closely allying the university and the health sector, with the aid of finance from the government department immediately concerned.

In all these examples, business and non-business alike, there can be seen the mixture of managerial interest and skills which is called for by the pressures of innovation. They exemplify the variety of influences which generate it and, in particular, the need for innovative thinkers, managers who will 'champion' innovation, and senior managers who will ensure that the resources are provided to carry it through. Some changes can take place, it is true, without involving top management: middle managers can sometimes make administrative changes of considerable importance without provoking policy issues. But major issues, certainly, require commitment to change at a number of levels – and the top level is crucial. The significance of individuals is also to be seen. Looking out from study of major companies like Du Pont, General Motors, and others, Professor Chandler remarks that the awareness of the needs and opportunities created by the changing environment seems to have depended on the training and personality of individual executives and on their ability to keep their eyes on the more important entrepreneurial problems even in the midst of pressing operational needs.[15]

The emphasis so far has been, to a considerable extent, on 'need input', often generated by buyers, and hence on marketing management. This has also been placed in the context of management as a whole. It should be remembered, however, that the same alertness to change is to be looked for in production, in organization and methods departments, and in other parts of management.

Professional and technical personnel[16]

In a conversation with the author a number of years ago, the managing director of a large pharmaceutical company discussed the problem of managing highly trained scientific personnel. He commented that they saw themselves as scientists rather than as businessmen or managers. It sometimes happened that their scientific output diminished after a time, that the company wanted to continue to use their abilities, and could only envisage doing so in a managerial capacity. This led to some resistance, he said, because the scientists regarded transition to management as a demotion. This is only a single anecdote, and one swallow does not make a summer. It does appear, however, that there are enough swallows to suggest that there may be genuine problems of this kind for management. Cotgrove and Box, writing in 1970, referred to 'the career problems' of middle-aged scientists, some of whom may be unsuited to administrative tasks, while others would in any case not wish to undertake them.[17] Their view was based on evidence collected from a considerable number of scientists, and especially from research management.

In organizations, moreover, which have a dominant or strong professional stream, the attitude to administration can have something of the flavour suggested above. Universities, and also hospitals, exemplify this. The work goals of academic staff will differ in certain critical respects from those of the administrative officers: the criteria by which academics evaluate others, and themselves, are related to their attitudes to their academic subjects, and to the judgement of their peers. It is not always easy to relate conditions to what the administrator, faced with budgetary and organizational constraints, may see as the management problems of the university. Writing about the internal organization of hospitals, Harris, who is both a clinician and an economist, has drawn attention to the management problem of resource allocation. Doctors have their requirements for each individual patient; administrators will doubtless tell them about the overall budgetary constraint.

Quinn and Mueller, in a paper aptly entitled 'Transferring Research Results to Operations', based on a study including interviews with over 200 top operating and research executives in the United States, were prepared to make this generalization:

Many researchers have been oriented by their training (and by country club environments) to regard research as a leisurely process, somehow abstracted from a 'crass' commercial world. Too frequently, they work almost casually on problems of tremendous competitive significance to the company or even to the country. Such researchers often want to pursue all the scientifically fascinating ramifications of a study, regardless of their relationship to the organization's goals. Research results appear slowly in these situations, and powerful frictions develop between research and operating groups.[18]

This view has been preceded by Quinn's references to the research director who 'shielded his researchers from "commercial pressures"' and to operating groups who had no information about important technical outcomes 'until those in research were "sure they would work"'. If one side of the coin is the 'seclusion' of research from operations, the other is the lack of knowledge among operating managers of the language of basic science and of technology.

It is just as well to be cautious about generalizations; indeed, there is evidence that what is true of the work goals of scientists may not apply in the same way to engineers. But there is enough information to indicate the existence of a management problem and a management task. The focusing of research effort on activities which will ultimately provide new products and processes which can be successfully marketed, the transfer of research results to commercial operation, and the integration of research and marketing strategy will not come about automatically. They have to be facilitated by managerial impulse and co-ordination. Professor Kanter argues, indeed, that the research departments themselves may have to be involved in the management process, since their managers have to persuade other managers to move into new product designs and other changes.

Research and development sometimes carry an aura around them; as Kanter says, 'I had somehow romanticized research-and-development departments, as non controversial havens for innovation . . .'.[19] This is another part of the seclusion of research from departments more closely associated with production and market operations and of the conflicts which may arise between research attitudes and commercial requirements. But the success of a research department, while it clearly depends on the quality of its research personnel, also depends on the skill with which it is managed and on the ability of its managers to make good their claims on the business budget. Those claims, as was seen above (and in Chapter 2 in looking at the individual's progress in management), must ultimately depend on the contribution of the activity to the economic requirements of the enterprises and have to be justified within that context.

All this is part and parcel of the recognition that innovation is a complex and time-consuming process which includes the implementation of ideas. The more radical the innovation, the less likely is it that it can be managed within the framework of existing procedures and organization and the more important will it be, therefore, that management should be geared towards the transfer of ideas into operations.

Types of innovation, success and failure

So far, the distinction between types of innovation has been rather loosely drawn, and it is, indeed, often difficult to draw very precise lines between different categories. From the point of view of products, Foxall points out, the question is: how do customers see the change, and what, in consequence, are the implications for product management? He finds it useful to cite Robertson's qualitative classification into:

- continuous innovations, i.e. marginal changes, of which fluoride toothpaste, enhanced chemical fertilizers are examples;
- dynamically-continuous innovations, such as electrically-powered lawn mowers, computer-aided design methods;
- discontinuous innovations, such as television, computers, video recorders.

Four important points emerge for management from this and similar classifications. One relates to uncertainty, which has been a pervasive theme in this book. The more discontinuous and radical the departure from existing product lines, the more has management to face up to uncertainty. Incremental change in the products which a business offers can be accommodated within existing procedures: it can, in other words, be routinized and programmed. Major innovations are, by definition, much more disturbing and disruptive of existing patterns of working and existing organizational relationships. A second point is that a large number of product innovations fail. This appears to be very strongly the case for consumer products, for example in the grocery trade, but the same general picture is true of industrial products. A number of products fail at the test-marketing stage, others at the national level. The damaging period in the innovative process appears to be the marketing stage. This enhances the importance of management relationships with the potential market, i.e. the customer. The third point is that the introduction of new products takes time. Consequently, as Foxall points out, citing the example of Ford's Edsel motor car in the 1950s as it advanced from idea to product, marketing managers may get customers' requirements right at the earliest stages, only to find that they have changed radically by the time the product comes on to the market.[20] This is no doubt obvious, but the recognition of the flow of time and the extent of the changes which can occur during the process of product development deserve emphasis because of their impact on management. A fourth point, therefore, is that managers may feel that in thinking about new product design they have to balance innovation plus uncertainty against imitativeness plus reasonable predictability. Hayes and Abernathy put the contrast in the form of a trade-off table[21]: see Figure 3.

FIGURE THREE

TRADE-OFFS BETWEEN IMITATIVE AND INNOVATIVE DESIGN
FOR AN ESTABLISHED PRODUCT LINE

Imitative design	*Innovative design*
Market demand is relatively well-known and predictable	Potentially large but unpredictable demand; the risk of a flop is also large
Market recognition and acceptance are rapid	Market acceptance may be slow initially, but the imitative response of competitors may also be slowed
Readily adaptable to existing market, sales, and distribution policies	May require unique, tailored marketing distribution and sales policies to educate customers or because of special repair and warranty problems
Fits with existing market segmentation and product policies	Demand may cut across traditional marketing segments, disrupting divisional responsibilities and cannibalizing other products

Hayes and Abernathy were writing in the context of the United States, but they were making, in effect, a general point: the incremental mode plays a very significant part in innovation. Interestingly enough, the incrementalism of Lindblom's analysis has a place in the management of innovation in business as well as on the larger stage of government and public administration. Yet there is a serious management problem here for the individual enterprise, if an innovative strategy and business organization appropriate to a stable environment encounter a reality of environmental turbulence in technology and competitive pressures. The idea of innovation presents management with its entrepreneurial as well as its ongoing aspect.

On organization and organizational innovation

Most of the discussion has been concerned with innovation in products and processes, and the direction of the argument about this extremely complex subject has been to show how interwoven it is with the responsibilities and abilities of management. It has been seen, also, that marketing strategy is a sub-set of the wider requirements of corporate strategy: thus Drucker thinks that innovation depends on answering the question 'What is our business to be?' There are also the questions 'What ought our organization to be?' and, specifically, 'What *organizational innovation* is required both to stimulate and to respond to the advantages of innovation?'

These topics can be dealt with only briefly here, and the main emphasis is on the management aspects, particularly in the large and *complex* business corporations and non-business organizations which have grown up over the last century. When a business, founded by an entrepreneur, grows in size and complexity – bigger sales, greater numbers employed, more capital invested, more product lines, geographical dispersal – it has to be managed by numbers of managers, and this, as Mariann Jelinek puts it, 'requires a shift from depending upon individual innovators to somehow generalizing and extending these abilities.'[22] Individual leaders or entrepreneurs often show a remarkable capacity for grasping and remembering detail and for exercising control: it is among their most distinctive qualities. But Jelinek is not alone in pointing out that the continued growth of any organization and its appetite for the innovation necessary to sustain it are bound to outstrip the powers of direction of any one person, however gifted that person may be. The reality of co-ordination and control, the volume and variety of information required to exercise them, will mean that numbers of members of the organization will, in practice, be contributing to the process and outcome.

The essence of this point is that somehow the abilities of individuals within an organization have to be brought together to generate innovation, which in the early days of the business was the province of one person or a few individuals. Since organizations as such do not think, or make decisions (see Chapter 7 below) – only individuals can do so – the problem is how to organize the structure and manage the relationship between people so as to achieve results.

Jelinek emphasizes the significance of having within a company the means for envisaging alternative futures. Management tends, naturally enough, to try to systematize what it has to do; to be systematic is to reduce the costs of learning. If there were no systematic set of rules and procedures for doing things, the managers would have to learn afresh every time they wanted to do anything. Moreover, people learn to be more efficient when they acquire skill in handling procedures, just as they enhance manual dexterity with practice in the use of tools. But established systems may not be suitable for detecting and acting on initiatives which lie outside the existing scope of the business. Incrementalist though many changes are, there are also many companies which undertake some form of corporate planning and which employ various methods, formal and informal, of directing attention towards large-scale change.

Some of these topics belong with the area of organization and are more fully discussed in Chapter 7. Innovation is typically associated with growth and diversity, which give rise to problems of decentralization and control. The oft-repeated emphasis on organizational flexibility is another crucial feature: is it possible for managers who are under the pressures of running the existing business to give adequate attention to considering the future business? How should that be arranged? In a rapidly changing environment, moreover, the introduction of the new has to be matched by decisions on when to discard the old. Different companies have different methods of tackling the problem of time to think, but perhaps one general lesson for management is expressed in a paper by Heller on Litton Industries (electronics, business equipment, etc.). He quotes Ash, the president of the company, as saying: 'We founded Litton on the theory that the end is to match technological innovation with equal skills by management, marketing and finance.'[23]

A concluding note on major innovations and unpredictability

Innovation is a large and complex theme and one in which it is very difficult to generalize about the behaviour of individual firms and organizations. Differences in type of industry, size of firm, current technological and competitive pressures, and managerial attitudes, all have something to do with the decisions made about research and innovation. They may all influence the balance between projects which are expected to pay off in the short or the long run, those which seem very risky, and those which seem tolerably predictable.

For major innovations, uncertainty and unpredictability are pervasive features of the manager's scene. Many managers, like many people, doubtless like to lean on their past experience and judgement and to move forward step-wise in the adoption of new products and technological processes.[24] This means continuous rather than discontinuous innovation. Professor Gold refers to the tendency, which uncertainty encourages, to eschew major innovations, so that it has often been the case that 'production and marketing innovations either had to be cut-down into bite-size experimental doses or face long delays.'[25] Of course, a decision process is a network of decisions; as was pointed out above, James Watt learned from the work of other people with whom he was friendly. In the same way it might be said that major innovations come about in a variety of ways, and that managers, even if cautious, come to adopt them when circumstances push them to a point of change and when, if possible, some testing has occurred elsewhere.

From the point of view of management critical features of innovation are the capacity to spot change, the ability to manage it both within the research and development function and in corporate management as a whole, and the need to relate product, process, and organizational change.

CHAPTER SEVEN

THE POLITICS OF ORGANIZATION: THE BUSINESS ENTERPRISE AS A SYSTEM OF GOVERNANCE

> Fail to honour people,
> They fail to know you;
> But of a good leader, who talks little,
> When his work is done, his aim fulfilled,
> They will all say, 'We did this ourselves.'

Lao Tzu, *The Way of Life: According to Lao Tzu*[1]

From early days, individuals live within the framework of organization, whether it be school or college or factory or office. Many of the decisions which affect their daily lives and welfare are made in organizations. How organizations work is, therefore, of tremendous importance. Decisions which shape the output of goods and services, the location of business activity, the demand for particular kinds of skill, are made within business corporations. Policies which affect the development of whole communities are made within government organizations. Everyday language is full of statements of the kind:

- The university has established a new faculty.
- The government has changed taxation.
- British Leyland have introduced a new car.
- Cadbury Schweppes have developed their interests in North America.

Textbooks in economics speak of 'the' firm or perhaps of 'the' entrepreneur.

But what is meant by saying that 'The university decided . . .' or that British Leyland or Cadbury Schweppes did something? How can 'the' university do anything, how can 'the' firm carry out any activity? Decisions have to be made by persons, not by institutions. So the statement that the organization did something is a kind of convenient shorthand which, translated, means the following:

- individual human beings, members of the university or of British Leyland etc. etc. held discussions, examined courses of action, made decisions in such a way that the end-result was a new faculty or a new car or . . .[2]
- such decisions are made in the framework of organization, which is not identical with individuals deciding their own personal affairs. The managers who make them have to have regard to their superiors, their peers, and their subordinates.

Thus, as was suggested earlier, the modern business corporation, which is often very large and complex, is in certain respects a system of governance, with a constitution, and with formal and informal conventions of government. That is why management can be envisaged as in the nature of a political process. This is one way, not the only way but a very important one, of interpreting the character and behaviour of organizations.

What is an organization?

The simplest answer to this question is that a formal definition of organizations is probably impossible. Such an answer given here is in good company. Arrow remarks: 'I am not going to attempt a formal definition of organizations, which would probably be impossible.'[3] Systems of classification imply a certain kind of tidiness which cannot always be found in the world; definitions imply a precision which cannot easily be provided, and it may be more productive, therefore, as March and Simon observe in their book entitled *Organizations*, to give examples of formal organizations rather than to try to fit them into a single definition.[4]

This is partly a matter of what is meant by a definition: ideally, it is something which covers a whole class of individuals, and the difficulty is that organizations are characterized by great variety. It could be very misleading to imagine that because the word organization applies to a school, a church, a business, a government department, they can all be analysed in precisely the same way. And yet if they are all organizations, it is to be expected that they will have features in common, features of sufficient importance to make possible significant generalizations applicable to all of them.

A very interesting example is the current discussion about university education in Britain, in which it has been argued that there is a cost-benefit equation to be considered. Value for money, it is held, is a major criterion for judging expenditure on universities, and value is expressed in terms of contribution towards improving the quality and competitive power of the British economy. When it is said that a business should be judged by its ability to supply products to markets which are willing to pay for them at prices which are profitable, nobody is noticeably startled. In fact, it would generally be supposed that a business is obliged to behave in that framework. But the proposition about universities as organizations, though perhaps less stark, provokes serious debate *about the nature of the institution*: what kind of organization is it, or should it be? The argument might be still more intense if applied to religious institutions: the balance sheet may be important, but a healthy balance sheet would not be regarded as the ultimate test of whether the institution had been doing the 'right' things.

To say, therefore, that a business enterprise, a church, or a university are all organizations is far from stating what they are: there are clearly considerable differences between them and in the criteria by which the management of them has to be assessed. Yet they do all have to be managed, and they have come to exist for reasons which can be classified. Leaving aside the question what exactly is an organization, it is possible to say: groups of people work in what are referred to as organizations, a term with which everyday language has comparatively little difficulty. They may not always be accustomed to thinking of a school as an organization, but they are quite comfortable in referring in this way to I C I, or Ford, or Tarmac, or Marks and Spencer, and they have no doubt that they know what they mean.

The questions are, therefore: why do the entities which are called organizations come into being, what purposes do they serve, and what characteristics do they possess? How do the activities of people in organizations differ from those which are conducted outside them, and does organization have a life of its own?

Consider first the related questions: why do organizations exist and what purposes are they believed to serve? The existence of organizations reflects the fact that some things can only be done by people working together, or can be done much better by working together than otherwise. A few simple examples will illustrate the point. If a man wishes to move a heavy piece of furniture which is beyond his own physical powers, he can engage either voluntary or paid help. If he employs casual paid help, he will have, in principle, to negotiate the price he has to pay each time he hires it. But if he has a frequent need to move heavy furniture, or thinks he may have, he may think it preferable to employ somebody regularly, who in return for a stipulated (weekly) wage is obliged to be available between agreed hours of work, to shift furniture as directed.

This small instance is a simplified version of the important proposition that 'The purpose of organizations is to exploit the fact that many (virtually all) decisions require the participation of many individuals for their effectiveness.'[5] Of course, the furniture mover does not have to employ somebody directly: he could enter into a contract with another individual. But once he does engage another person, in other words, once a contractual employment relationship has been established, an embryonic organizational form has been created and a management situation will exist. The further implication of this proposition is that

Transactions that take place within organizations, far more than in markets, are preplanned and precoordinated. The automobile engine division knows exactly how many engine blocks to put into production – not because it has made a forecast of the market, but because its production plan has been coordinated with the plans for producing completed automobiles in other departments of the company.[6]

Organization, in other words, is associated with co-ordination and planning (see Chapter 9 below). The example of engine blocks is not really different, in principle, from the small instance of furniture removal, since there may very well be a choice of buying in components rather than making them. The important point is contained in the phrases 'preplanned and precoordinated' and 'its production plan has been coordinated with . . .'. Formal organization is a device for utilizing the contributions of numbers of people whose participation is needed to achieve the required purposes and whose activities are co-ordinated by means of a planning process.

It can be seen, also, that organization is a means of dealing with uncertainty and unpredictability. The engine division knows how many engine blocks to produce: the users of engine blocks know that the engine division is committed to the required level of production, and that, provided it does its job, the parts will turn up as 'preplanned'. Similarly, the establishment of an organization *structure* enables members to know who is dealing with what topics, who has to be given what information, and so on. The idea of organization is, in a manner of speaking, to compensate for the fact that human beings are neither perfect nor perfectly alike, and that it requires the participation of different people to achieve purposes by working in unison. How they are brought to do so despite their differences is the story of the linking factor between organization and accomplishment: that link is called management. The relationships are both formal and informal; within the formal structure, experience is built up which forms part of the cultural identity of an organization and constitutes what may be called a shared reality among its members. This phrase is discussed more fully later on; it refers to that kind of understanding among members of an organization about what is acceptable and what is not, what is done and what is not done. Two practical examples will show how important this is in the management context.

1. In Thomas Tilling, both the chief executive of the time and the managing director of one of the major subsidiaries spoke, independently, of 'trust' as the basis of management relationships. There were conventions about the respect shown for subordinates, for example, which *were allowed to* override the *formal* rights of superiors.

2. Mr Hugh Norton of British Petroleum, speaking at the time as its Director of Planning, referred to the problem of cultural unity when the company changed its organizational structure in the wake of its programme of diversification.

Like most institutions [he said], companies have their 'cultures', styles and esprits de corps. These may sometimes be derided, but they do help to preserve the unity of an organization and give it ethos. In a diversified company the loss of cultural unity is probably inevitable: the question is, should senior managers try and create a new corporate style, or should they let each business stream develop in its own way?[7]

These examples illustrate, firstly, that the line between formal and informal is not always easy to draw in organizations: that is one reason why it is so difficult to define the term 'a formal organization'. Secondly, they show that the informal understandings and customs which are built up through time contribute to the reduction of uncertainty referred to above, by establishing a set of expectations about what is acceptable or otherwise within the organization.

Obviously, the fact that defining an organization may be impossible does not mean that organizations do not exist; nor does it mean that there is no commonsense way of understanding them. A person who says 'I work for company X' or 'I work for Y university' is quite able to recognize boundaries of responsibility and authority. It is useful to emphasize, however, that organizations are not tidy systems closed to the outside world, nor are the relationships between their members solely a matter of formal rules and procedures.

So far in this section the emphasis has been on organization as a planning device and as a mode of dealing with uncertainty by developing standardized forms. But a further aspect is that an organization is a means of securing a kind of 'immortality' or, at least, continuity. In an organized business enterprise or a university or school or hospital, what organization makes possible is the continued performance of tasks and pursuit of goals, irrespective of the presence of particular individuals. The success of any one organization may depend, at least in part, on the ability and style of individual personalities, but *in principle* one managing director can (and eventually will) be succeeded by another. The same applies at other levels of the organization, because the individuals who participate in organization do so in a role or functional capacity, e.g. as marketing managers, or chief accountants, or sales representatives, or professors . . . and not simply as individuals. When it is sometimes said that organizations consist of people, the statement is incomplete. A large crowd milling about in busy streets or in large stores is not an organization: people in organizations are bound together by functions they fulfil, tasks they perform, and purposes they pursue. Wilfred Brown dealt with this point in terms of what he treated as the *executive system*,

the structure of roles more commonly referred to as the organization chart of hierarchy (including operators, clerks, etc., as well as managers or executives). It exists irrespective of people. Individuals may come and go but the role does not disappear. New roles can be added to the system before any thought is given to who should fill them. The work content of roles can increase or decrease in importance without the persons in the roles changing their personal capacity to do the work. Because this social structure exists as an entity in itself it can be consciously thought about and altered.[8]

These are substantial points for students of organization and the management process. They underline the idea of the continuity of organization and also its malleability: managers design it and managers can remould it (although that may not be easy). There is one cautionary note which should be entered: it is true, as Brown holds, that roles exist independently of individuals, but not absolutely so. The way individuals interpret their roles may greatly influence the content and meaning of the roles, so that the same position occupied by different persons may become almost a different job.

Organizations and objectives

Human behaviour in organizations is purposive, that is to say, it is aimed at achieving objectives. That may seem so obvious as hardly to need saying, but it is important to say it, nevertheless, in order to explain what is meant by objectives in organizations. Just as it was argued above that organizations cannot make decisions – only individuals can do so – it can also be said that organizations cannot have objectives – only the members of the organization can have them. And yet it is perfectly customary and comprehensible to say that company X aims at a particular share of the market, or level of return, or annual growth rate. Everyday language is not to be despised, so it is necessary to look at these different statements and try to examine what they mean.

Consider, to start with, an example of the kind of general proposition which companies sometimes advance. Sir Halford Reddish, speaking at a seminar on the theme of the Rugby Portland Cement Company, of which he was chairman, said that it was company policy never to dismiss an employee provided that that employee was performing his duties as required. Only in acute circumstances would the company lay off employees for any reason other than failure to do the job required, and at the time of speaking Sir Halford said they had never come to that point. He saw this as a policy parameter, an obligation imposed on the company (by itself). Whether this can be called a company goal is perhaps open to dispute, but it certainly makes sense to say that this was the policy of the Rugby Portland Cement Company.

The point may be put in a general way. It is customary in economic theory to refer to the firm, to say that it seeks to maximize profits or sales, or to attain some other objective. This terminology might give the impression that a firm is a real person in the sense that 'it' thinks and does things. But strictly speaking, to say that firms maximize profits or would like to do so must be understood to mean 'that the *people who run firms* make decisions so as to maximize the profits of firms.' [9]

This is another form of the view expressed earlier, that statements about what an organization does are shorthand expressions for a whole network of management procedures and decisions. Now when Reddish spoke of company policy, this could have been interpreted in various ways, e.g. 'This is *my* policy for Rugby Portland' or 'This is the board's policy' or 'This is the policy favoured by senior managers and which the board has agreed to pursue.' Similarly, the phrases about maximizing profit are statements about what people are seeking to do.

There are further points, however, which are of even greater importance for an understanding of the management function. In any organization there are multiple goals, and this multiplicity of goals follows from two facts: one is that even individuals have more than one goal; the second is that different groups have different objectives because they look at the organization from different perspectives. Junior managers will view career questions differently from middle managers; a sales department, wanting something which it is good to sell, or a production department something convenient to make, will differ from a research department, which uses resources for future purposes rather than current output.

The consequence of this multiplicity of goals is that an organization is, as was pointed out earlier, the scene of goal conflict. There is nothing inherently nasty about this: conflict may be translated as 'imperfect compatibility', meaning that it is not feasible to satisfy all goals one hundred per cent all the time. The success of an organization does not depend, however, on eliminating differences but on the capacity to arrive at agreed courses of action in spite of differences. Thus an essential feature of management is the management of conflict: for if everybody saw eye to eye on every single issue, on every possible interpretation of events, and on every anticipated change of direction, what would be the real difficulty of the manager's task? It has already been noted in the discussion of decision-making that there will typically be more than one possible decision which would make sense. Similarly, there may be more than one way of resolving disagreements and more than one view of acceptable solutions.

Is this too complicated a view of goals? Might not a top manager say 'I know very well what we are aiming at: it is to maximize earnings per share' or 'to make our company the biggest in the country in its line of business'? But it is clear enough that there will be other purposes: for instance, to maintain levels of quality or, as in the Reddish example, to meet a self-defined standard of security of employment. So it is by no means an entirely straightforward matter even in the case of business; it is likely to be more difficult in the case of universities or churches, where the scope of generalization is even wider. Consider the statement which is sometimes made about academic institutions (and by them about themselves), that they aim to be centres of excellence. This kind of terminology is quite often used and it has merit as a general indication of the standard by which the institution is to be judged – and by which it will judge its own decisions. But what exactly does it mean in practice? How will teaching, research, administrative ability, be judged as contributors to excellence? What will be the standards of comparison? Who decides how these general ideas are to be translated into practical courses of action?

There is another question to be considered: how is it possible to know what the goals of an organization are – how would this be discovered? Some organizations set out their purposes in writing: Hewlett-Packard in the United States, for example, has a 'Statement of Corporate Objectives'; the aims of nationalized industries in Britain were set out in the nationalizing legislation and in speeches by ministers in the House of Commons when the legislation was under consideration there. But of course what is written down or stated cannot always be taken at face value, not because of any deliberate obfuscation, but because it may only reflect what was true at a particular time and, especially, because the test of those statements only really comes when choices have to be made about what to do in a given situation. In other words, while general statements about the goals or objectives of an organization are important because they set the scene for management and help establish the 'cultural climate', the problem of management is to set and work to *operative goals or objectives*. That means, the objectives which actually guide the operations of the organization: for example, if an academic institution has a general aim of being a centre of excellence, what criteria will it use for appointing staff to academic posts? One interesting instance is given by R. H. Hall, who refers to the faculty information booklet of an American university which listed the aims of excellent teaching, research, community service, etc.

But were these aims of equal weight in making decisions about academic staff? In practice not, despite the impression conveyed by the formal statement in the booklet. The critical test of what really counts is what happens when decisions have actually to be made, as Hall suggests in a specific example of salary increases. When these were under review for the next year, the members of at least one department in the university were asked how many offers had been made to them by other universities – a market measure, so to speak. The answer to this question was, it appears, the most relevant factor in the decision, and since most offers came to individuals who were strong in research (because outside universities could judge this more easily), the research goal acquired a special weight, *from an operative point of view*.[10]

In business also, if perhaps to a lesser degree, similar considerations arise. A company may be interested in a variety of objectives, profit, growth, quality of products; how they are traded off against one another is part of the decision process. If an objective is stated that the company seeks profitability, what *specific* objectives does that involve?

Hall takes the view, to which Quinn has also pointed in his extensive study of business enterprises, that those specific objectives, which are the operative goals of an organization, will be reflected in the decisions which are actually made. What the top decision-makers decide about the use of resources, human and material, is the story of what they are doing. More than that, it records the objectives to which they are in practice working; what they do codifies what they are aiming at. These operative goals will usually differ to some extent from the general stated aims of the organization, but will be drawn from them. They will no doubt be reasonably closely related to those general aims which may indeed be regarded as points of reference or appeal: the operative decisions might well come to form a body of case law.[11]

What conclusions can be drawn from this, particularly with respect to the theme of organization as a system of governance and to management implications? One is that there are purposes and objectives – that behaviour in organizations is not just a series of random responses to circumstances or stimuli. A second is that general goals have importance, but the test arises when decisions have to be made in terms of operative goals. A third point is that it is individuals who have goals, not collectivities: but individuals in organizations are not identical with individuals pursuing personal objectives. They have to focus on the organization and on their organizational relationship with other members of it. This was expressed in Simon's remark, mentioned earlier, about decision-making, that the executive has one eye on the matter in hand, the other on its organizational consequences. Fourthly, because goals are multiple, differences and conflicts and the need to deal with them are inherent in the very nature of organization. The multiplicity of goals stems partly from the varying perceptions of the different departments in the organization as in any societal system. The relationships, formal and informal, between the departments constitute a system which has to be governed. There are established rules and unwritten conventions which form the constitution of an organization, and which have to be observed as far as possible. This applies to the balancing of the legitimate but conflicting objectives which have to be reconciled. This is the business of management.

Thus, managers are not people who simply concern themselves with the external environment, crucial though that is. They spend much of their time (sometimes they must feel too much) on the *internal* management of the organization – discussing, negotiating, bargaining, persuading – so that the organization can be maintained as an effective vehicle for the performance of tasks which require the participation of many individuals and units. For the objective of survival of the organization is crucial: indeed, it has been argued that it is perhaps the one objective, if there were only one, which can be detected. One important element in this picture of the process is that objectives have to be *discovered* and *established*. The picture of objectives as *given*, so that management has only to be concerned with achieving them, is unrealistic. Managers have to decide which objectives to pursue, which are feasible and which are not, and to change objectives whenever appropriate.

Purposes, information, and organization

Hitherto, the emphasis of this chapter has been on multiple purposes. Some writers would go to the extent of saying, indeed, that there is no such thing as a common purpose: that the effectiveness of a business or non-business organization depends on the existence of *joint* purposes. This is an important point which warrants some exploration. The argument would run like this: in order to make organization worthwhile and effective, it is not necessary for the members to have a common purpose or set of purposes. It is only necessary that they should find that their separate purposes are better satisfied by working in unison with others than by working in isolation. The task of management, as has already been observed, is to keep those joint purposes together.

There is a great deal to be said for that point of view, and, general and abstract though it may appear, it does in fact fit very well with the work that managers have to perform. But it goes too far, because there can be overriding values and purposes to which members of organizations give their acceptance even if they do not interpret them identically (since individuals are not identical). Perhaps the more effective phrase would be that there are shared purposes which are recognized as standards of reference against which operative goals are assessed. Another point in this context is that members of an organization may have different views about its goals but may be able to agree on the procedures for dealing with them. Two people may disagree fundamentally on, say, the question of restoration of capital punishment but can be content to agree that the decision should be made (in Britain) by Parliament. Or two members of a faculty may hold different opinions on subjects to be included in a degree programme but can be content to agree that the outcome should be decided by a particular committee and by an established procedure. Managers may differ on some aspect of, say, quality standards or sales promotion, but can accept that the result should be decided in a particular management committee.

It is clear that different members of an organization may place different emphasis on various objectives even where they may all agree on the relevance of the objectives. This makes it very important to draw attention to the question of acceptance of objectives. If the organization is to survive, it must have sufficient coherence, i.e. there has to be that *shared reality* to which reference has already been made. Members of an organization, whether they be managers in a business enterprise or, say, academic staff in a university, are in some sense members of a community, which means that they are prepared positively to support, or at the least, to 'go along with' the ostensible objectives and the operative decisions which embody those objectives. It is worth bearing in mind, moreover, that even if individuals are not always absolutely clear about objectives, they may very well know what is unacceptable to them. For example, they may not be sure about the share of the market at which the company should aim, but they may be quite clear that the existing share is not high enough.

How far is this idea of acceptance a valid picture of reality in organizational life, faced with the part played by hierarchy and authority? Consider the following example from a large public organization which was at the time subject to stringent constraints: difficulties with sales, pressures on its costs. The various parts of the business were set targets by the upper levels of the management: 'top down' targets. The lower, though still senior, echelons had their own views on targets: 'bottom up'. They recognized the authority of top management and were consequently prepared to do their best to meet the 'top down' requirements. But there is no doubt that they were sceptical – 'If that's what they want they had better come here and tell us how they think it can be done' – that they expressed this scepticism to top management, and that their attitude was seen to be important.

The term 'acceptance' is an elastic one. In this example, the authority and the targets were accepted as the formal requirements: the acceptance of authority is, after all, part of the contract of employment. The limits to this acceptance, however, were the lack of conviction at the lower levels about the real feasibility of the targets and, on the other hand, the fact that what was required by top management was not so drastic as to be too repugnant to the lower (senior) levels. What this implies is that management has not merely to exercise authority but also to recognize what are the effective bounds of its authority and the limits of the power which may wisely be exercised. Members of an organization, even if they have little or no significant positive power at their levels, may respond by failure to comply or by withdrawal – although they may be able to do so only at considerable cost. Hence the emphasis placed by some top executives on the need to carry their managers with them in the decision process. This is the element of consent.[12]

There is a conceptual spectrum from a rigid absolutism to pure consensus; Loasby thinks that there is some limit to authority even at the rigid end. An element of authority, similarly, will temper the purest consensus. If the real situations lie between the two, then the conditions which managers experience will be those of a negotiated environment. This need not mean formally negotiated in every respect but one in which both formal and informal understandings establish a balance of relationships among the different layers of management.

This analysis closely parallels the discussion of decision-making in Chapter 3 and, like that discussion, it raises the topic of information. For it is information which fuels the movement of an organization by making clear to its members what the objectives are and by constituting the input of which decisions are the output . . . commitments to courses of action. In a sense, an organization can be regarded as a set of information channels which take in and transmit information, and convert it into outputs of goods and services. The questions to which managers have to give answers are: what information do we have, what information do we need, what do we do with the information we possess, and, critically, *what is the meaning of the information we have*? Managers are, in other words, acquirers, users, and *interpreters* of information.

Organizations and information

Many basic textbooks on management give a great deal of attention to the importance of information and communications; in this section, the focus is on the link between organization and the use of information.

In order to take effective action, managers must have both a certain amount of knowledge and also the possibility of acquiring more. They need to be able to receive information and to transmit it to other members of the organization. The value of the information consists in its capacity to make action possible and to improve the quality of actions taken. 'Decisions,' as Kenneth Arrow says, 'are necessarily a function of information.'[13] Why is this important in the study of organization? To begin with, in Simon's words,

Only in the case where the man who is to carry out a decision is also the man best fitted to make that decision is there no problem of communication – and in this exceptional case there is of course no reason for organization. In all other cases means must be devised for transmitting information from its organizational sources to decisional centers, from centers where component decisions are made to centers where these are combined, and from the latter to the points in the organization where the decisions are to be carried out.[14]

A further reason is that not everybody needs nor can everybody have all the information all the time. If every member of an organization, every manager, were to pass on every detail of information that he received, the process would be extremely costly in time, effort and physical resources. What cost advantages could accrue to organization in these circumstances? Consider, also, that the value of information depends on the ability of the receiver to comprehend and to act on it; but in every organization, there are necessarily specialists in particular fields, alongside others who do not have that degree of special knowledge. Thus, what happens in reality is that managers in an organization sift information before they pass it along; they summarize it and decide that some information is irrelevant to the decision and can therefore be safely omitted. And although this summarizing may be a danger-point in any organization, it is also vital, for without it no economies can be gained from the organization of the information process.

There are two ways of expressing this. Organization is a means of securing and channelling information and is required because it economizes on the data used at each point of decision. Irrelevant information is discarded somewhere along the way. It has been said that the hierarchy in an organization acts as an information filter in that each level passes upwards only what it regards as relevant to the higher level. 'The organization is thus an apparatus mainly set up to shield the executive from information.'[15] This is a matter of good sense in the use of managerial resources, since clearly the chief executive of a company does not need to receive detailed information on each machine in a factory; the chairman of a bank does not need to be given a detailed record of the weekly transactions of a particular small account in one of the branches. The argument also cuts the other way: the chief executive or chairman does not need to be concerned with telling each machine operator or bank cashier what to do in every particular instance. This does not mean that the senior managers never deal with any kind of detail: it means that they do not cover every kind of detail and that they have a primary concern with general matters and instructions.

Since decisions depend on information and since information is filtered and summarized as it enters and is transmitted through the organization, the channels of transmission and the quality of the managers are fundamental aspects of effective and efficient behaviour. This applies both to external information, i.e. about the external environment, and to internal information, i.e. about what is going on *inside* the organization. What is happening in the economy at large, what factors which affect the enterprise are changing and how, how is the company performing in sales, profits, market share? Internally, which members of staff are doing well, what requirements are there for new staff, which functions require strengthening, what is being done about management training? It is obvious that a great variety of information is accumulated but that by no means all of it can be called 'hard fact'.

Consider an example from a non-business environment. A university administration, faced with the prospect of a reduction in its financial grant, prepared a detailed budget statement for the consideration of the senate, showing, with 'hard' figures, that the consequence of the cutback would be a deficit on a year of £x million by a specified date. This information had been prepared by careful and conscientious officers of the university; but when it was presented to the senate, the reaction of many members was to *query* the information. Were there not other data about the university's assets which would be relevant to decisions, and which had been sifted out? Were the 'hard' figures to be depended on? For example, the figures for anticipated revenues and expenditures of the university depended on *assumptions* about the likely trend of interest rates and inflation, and there were differences of opinion about the assumptions.

This example is clearly pertinent to the problem of planning in large organizations and is discussed more fully in Chapter 9 below. It emphasizes here that within an organizational framework information may be a· matter of debate and interpretation, partly because it is viewed from varying perspectives. One point·which has been underlined in this book, especially in Chapter 2, is that managers are frequently faced with the problem of making sense of expert information in a number of fields in which they themselves are not experts. Now information can be regarded as a series of signals: the simplest form of signal is a traffic light which tells motorists something about traffic flows. Statistics showing a drop in sales of a product signal something to a firm – exactly what, is a matter which has to be interpreted. To be able to receive signals means learning a language: signals in French can only be received by somebody whose native tongue it is, or who has invested time, effort and money in acquiring it. Similarly, any particular expertise, accounting, marketing, operations research, etc., has to be learned; thus the capacity to receive signals requires an investment in learning, either by the individual or by the organization for its members.

Inside an organization, therefore, the ability to receive, process, transmit and utilize information represents a kind of fixed capital both in terms of the physical equipment involved – which may be substantial and costly – and of the investment in learning relevant languages. The latter may well be the more significant factor. Just as with other forms of capital, an organization may be very reluctant to jettison something on which so much has already been spent. This applies to the formal structure of information which is set up in an organization and to the informal means by which knowledge is communicated from one person to another. Informality, curiously enough, can be a matter of organization: the senior common room and the executive dining room are cases in point. It is also a matter of shared experience, built up, perhaps, over a long period of time.

Two quotations will underline the analysis:

Communication is not a secondary or derived aspect of organization – a 'helper' of the other presumably more basic functions. It is rather the essence of organized activity and is the basic process out of which all other functions derive.

and

Communication in organization . . . is not a *means* of organization. It is the *mode* of organization.[16]

The whole of the economic process is about the transmission and appreciation of information, and the essence of effective and efficient processes is that the appropriate information should be transmitted in the appropriate quantities to the point of decision. A market mechanism, for example, is a subtle device for conveying critical information to buyers; a consumer who wants to buy foodstuffs or clothing clearly has to know about prices. But the consumer cannot know and does not need to know all about the production processes employed in manufacturing them. In a business enterprise or a non-business organization the information process has to be consciously designed by management: who requires what kind of information, how shall it be transmitted, what feedback mechanisms should exist to ensure that decisions and actions materialize as the end-products of information?

All this illustrates the point frequently made here, that it is partial ignorance and inherent uncertainty which make the manager's task what it is. Information is not free, and because costs in time and money are incurred in obtaining and using it, managerial decision is involved to determine how much information is worth having and how much of it should be transmitted to which members of the system. This is clearly important in business planning, but its link with organization is admirably demonstrated in examples cited by Kennedy and Payne:

two innovations in cost control in the 1920s [they write] gave General Motors a substantial advantage over Ford in their struggle for dominance in the US automobile industry. One was the careful systematic comparison of unit costs in different GM plants. This helped keep average costs in GM plants very close to lowest costs and may have permitted 'super-fast' diffusion of new manufacturing techniques. This cost-comparison method was made possible only by the reorganization of the firm on the basis of autonomous divisions all using a uniform set of accounting conventions.

The second innovation to which Kennedy and Payne refer is that

GM's management, by putting dealer inventory reports on a ten-day rather than monthly basis, and by giving such reports the highest priority, elevated this tool into a much more powerful control mechanism. This practice also had the advantage, given GM's spread of products over the entire automotive range, of heightening the sensitivity of management to market trends and allowing the best use to be made of raw material stocks and accessory production.[17]

These examples (which suggest, incidentally, that the study of business history might be a very valuable element in the development of senior managers) show that the type of information available can closely affect competitive economic performance and that the *availability* of information depended on organizational innovation. The management question is not just 'What information shall we gather?' but also 'How should we be organized so as to be able to gather, and to utilize, useful information?' This is especially true of the first example, in which the main clue to success was the creation of autonomous divisions. The questions cut both ways: thus, for example, management might ask 'What information would be required to enable divisions to be autonomous?' A business organized on a national basis might face just that problem, if it were considering the problem of devolution. And the same principle applies inside organizations, business and non-business alike, whenever the questions of centralization and decentralization are considered (see Chapter 8 below).

The managers of large enterprises may very well be faced with problems of this kind, as two further examples will demonstrate. Consider a business such as the postal system in Britain. This is organized nationally, regionally, and with numbers of head postmasters responsible for areas and activities of varying size and complexity. How should the effectiveness and efficiency of the business be judged in respect, say, of a large city? Should it be regarded as a cost centre or profit centre, and if so, what information would be required? The questions of what is the most suitable policy (which is not the issue being discussed here), the system of control, and the availability of necessary information go together. Some kinds of organization may be possible only if appropriate information can be provided, and thus some forms may be impossible because information is not available. The second example is one which is discussed from time to time in a university context, and it is also concerned with the relationship between the central administration and the separate faculties. What information flow would be required in order to make possible, say, increased autonomy of the faculties in decisions about allocation of resources? Some departments in universities have separate financial budgets: if this idea were to be extended, what information and control mechanisms would have to be supplied?

It can be seen, then, that the study of information problems is bound up with the form of organization and, therefore, with the question of management control.

Responsibility, accountability and control

When an organization is created, it means that advantage can be taken of division of labour, that is to say, of specialization. This can take the form of employing individuals who, because of their special training and skills, can provide expert contributions in particular aspects of an organization, such as finance, marketing, production engineering etc., and of the creation of whole departments concerned with those aspects. An organization also has a hierarchy in which levels of authority are established. These two features raise three main matters for management in all enterprises, and especially in the large and complex modern corporation.

The first is concerned with the lateral co-ordination of departments whose heads are of equal status. A great deal of discussion about management is concerned with relationships between higher and lower levels of authority and power. But for its effective functioning a modern business requires means of securing co-operation between departments which are at the same level but which may look at things from varying perspectives. This lateral network is a pervasive and important characteristic of modern enterprises.

The second feature is the problem of responsibility and account-ability, which is bound to be important wherever there has been some element of delegation and decentralization. In a sense, any organi-zation can be envisaged as a system of responsibilities and account-abilities. Thus, for example, a marketing manager at the head of a marketing department may be *responsible* for all the activities which have been assigned to the department: may be *accountable* to a group marketing director to whom there is explicit requirement to report. *Ultimate* responsibility will in turn rest with the managing director (or board of directors) to whom the marketing director is accountable. The argument might, of course, be extended beyond the board of directors, who could be said to be accountable to the general body of shareholders or, in a nationalized industry, to Parliament through a minister.

The third aspect is the problem of control in organizations. The very fact that managers may be free to use their own discretion, in other words to exercise their own judgement, is what gives rise to the need for control. At first sight, this may seem paradoxical, since, surely, it is a strictly centralized, tightly disciplined organization which can best be described as controlled. Exact rules and regulations will tell individuals what they must or must not do, and their behaviour and responses will be known because they are precisely prescribed. This can be seen, for example, in a good deal of the work of disciplined services such as a fire or prison service; and there, perhaps, the most important control is the feedback mechanism which checks that the rules are being observed. (Ideally, of course, the system would work like clockwork, though this it never quite does.)

All this is true, but what is here being described is in fact a regulated mechanism which has to be administered. It is particularly apt in disciplined or repetitive activities where accurate, habituated response is crucial. But a genuine question of how to control is much more in evidence in those circumstances and in those decision-making situations where managers have been given freedom to make their own judgements. For it is then that higher levels of management will require to know that delegated decisions are compatible with what they see as the requirements of the organization as a whole. They will want to know, positively, that what needs doing is being done; negatively, that things are not being done contrary to what they would wish. In these circumstances, controls establish the parameters within which discretion may be exercised. In other words, since it is not feasible to give *absolute* discretion nor, as Loasby has argued, to have *absolute* control, the management problem is how to reconcile, or to balance, the twin considerations of decentralized initiative with management control.

The three aspects outlined above have been the subject of an enormous literature in organization studies, and the problems which arise are at the heart of management decisions and management practice. Inevitably, there are many different views and ways of doing things: some of them reflect varied opinions and experience, others are a result of different circumstances. Firms differ in size, technology, markets, personnel, and in their history. Again, what is applicable to the management of a business enterprise need be by no means applicable to a church, school, university, hospital or prison. Whereas, for example, many industrialists (and academics) regard the management and control of diversified companies as one of the most difficult tasks and hence emphasize that diversification is best confined to related fields, Sir Patrick Meaney at Thomas Tilling put much more stress on the problem of excessive size of individual units than on diversity. He thought that if numbers employed in a particular location exceeded about five hundred, it tended to create serious difficulties in communication and control. Or again, for example, whereas in a business environment control is essentially concerned to influence performance at work, a church wishes to influence behaviour not only during attendance at services but also outside them.

Nevertheless, in the great variety of situations there are some common threads which ought to be recognized for purposes of management, and they can be set out almost as a set of illustrated principles.

1. Responsibility, in the sense in which the term is used here, is something which cannot be abdicated. At each level of management, the manager who has been given responsibility is committed to it. The remarkable words of Winston Churchill quoted on p. 25 and the homely statement that 'The buck stops here' exemplify this point. An interesting example from industry of how responsibility might be exercised was given by John Neville, as chief executive of Manganese Bronze, discussing the relationship between top management at the centre of the business and its subsidiary companies. He believed that once a board of directors of a subsidiary company in the group had been entrusted with responsibility for running it, they must be left to do so. It was a matter for their judgement; but headquarters could not divest itself of ultimate responsibility for setting general policy and strategic parameters for the group. Moreover, if the senior management of a subsidiary did not do its job well, did not meet what was requried of it, there was the ultimate sanction that it could be replaced by other directors. Something not dissimilar was expressed by the top men in the major construction company Tarmac, who said that the group had, as one mode of control, the appointment of the senior executives who ran the divisions.

2. Accountability is the other side of the responsibility coin. It is a critical feature in the structure of control, since it is difficult to see, for example, how a manager who is not accountable to anybody can

be said to be under any form of control. It is also important to note that absence of accountability is a fruitful source of mistakes, since there is less challenge to individuals to justify their actions.

3. While control is often seen, as everyday language suggests, as some mechanism by which performance is measured against a standard, and a means by which members of an organization are brought to comply with standards, the word can also be interpreted as co-ordination. This applies to hierarchical control throughout the levels of the organization but especially to the lateral network, to try to ensure that what is being done in marketing a firm's product, for example, is matched by appropriate decisions in production and inventory. Co-ordination of this kind may be secured in a variety of ways: a management committee in which the separate plans of departments are discussed is one obvious method.

4. Control is necessitated by the existence of delegation, and this raises rather special questions about the appropriate nature of management controls, particularly at higher levels of an organization. There is a reason for this, which is connected with the earlier analysis of knowledge and bounded rationality. Because there are limits on the knowledge which it is possible for individuals to have, and because decisions are made in an uncertain environment, one of the tasks of management control is to try to stabilize uncertainty. One way of doing this is to introduce standardized procedures: another is to limit the area of uncertainty with which particular managers and departments have to deal. In other words, specialization is a method of coping with uncertainty because it demarcates the area of knowledge which is required and keeps it within manageable bounds. At the same time, the form of control at senior levels may take the form of setting limits and general targets. A characteristic limit is on the amount of capital expenditure which may be made by a division of an enterprise without detailed higher authorization; targets might be expressed as sales volume or rates of return.

There is one striking consequence for managers of this emphasis on responsibility. Since managers have responsibility for tasks and decisions which have been delegated to others, and since they cannot be constantly familiar, at every moment of the day, with how these are being accomplished, they are carrying responsibility for the possible mistakes of others and without complete knowledge. It might be said in fact that while a manager is not to blame for a particular fault, he nevertheless may carry responsibility for it. Hence responsibility and control are allies, since controls monitor performance, enable managers to take corrective action, and thus to discharge their responsibilities.

Organization and governance

In this concluding section of the chapter, it is now possible to take up the basic idea that an organization, business or otherwise, can be seen as a system of governance, with some of the properties of a constitutional machinery, and the behaviour patterns of a political system. The ways in which such a system functions, the demands it makes on managers, and the qualities in them which it calls for are clearly very important factors in selection and training. This aspect, although not unique to them, is perhaps especially significant in organizations which are both large and complex, i.e. which employ many people and large amounts of capital, have large sales turnover, and are multi-product and multi-market.

In a striking passage, Selznick discusses the management of conflict in these terms:

Internal interest groups form naturally in large-scale organizations, since the total enterprise is, in one sense, a polity composed of a number of suborganizations. The struggle among competing interests always has a high claim on the attention of leadership. This is so because the direction of the enterprise as a whole may be seriously influenced by changes in the internal balance of power. In exercising control, leadership has a dual task. It must win the consent of constituent units, in order to maximize voluntary cooperation, and, therefore, must permit emergent interest blocs a wide degree of representation. At the same time, in order to hold the helm, it must see that a balance of power appropriate to the fulfillment of key commitments will be maintained.[18]

Selznick is writing about leadership in administration, but his words have a wide applicability to problems of management: they can be supplemented by Pettigrew's study of organizational decision-making, in which he says that

the organization is considered an open political system. The division of work in an organization creates sub-units. These sub-units develop interests based on specialized functions and responsibilities. Although such sub-units have specialized tasks, they may also be interdependent. This interdependence may be played out within a joint decision-making process.[19]

The 'political' aspect of these propositions is that the sub-units will make demands on scarce resources in the organization and will seek to generate support for those demands or claims. It is the relationship between the sub-units, and between the sub-units and the organization as a whole in respect of these, which require political understanding and political skills in management. It engages the managers in the array of balancing, negotiating and trade-off activities which are implicit in the decision-making process of complex organizations.

These statements contain a number of key words and phrases which become practical guidelines for management. What both writers are saying can be expressed in a simplified chart: see Figure 4.

FIGURE FOUR

ORGANIZATION AS POLITY

An organization is	
a polity	a 'political' entity or system of administration and management
a political entity	has separate interest groups
separate interest groups	means that any polity has sub-units
sub-units make claims on overall scarce resources	hence there is conflict of claims
and sub-units try to gain support for their claims	how are these sub-units to be managed within the overall framework?

Now consider some of those phrases in Figure 4. To begin with, any organization may have a variety of entirely legitimate interest groups – which may be overlapping. In a business, for example, it was noted earlier that there are the separate interests or perspectives of different functional departments: sales looking for products which have strong selling attractiveness, production concerned with manufacturing facilities, research and development arguing that its work is the seed corn for the future of the company. In a university, different departments within a faculty, and different faculties within the university as a whole, will have views on which areas should receive priority in staffing and other resources. The same applies in other organizations, and each separate group will 'fight its corner'. Overlapping may occur because there are other kinds of interest group, such as junior managers compared with middle or senior managers, lecturers compared with professors, and so on.

There need be nothing sinister in these differences of interest, for they only tell us that an organization is a pluralist society. Nor need there be a sinister interpretation of the term 'conflict', which, it has already been seen, can be translated as 'imperfect compatibility'. This only reflects the fact that members of an organization are individuals with different opinions, working in departments, sub-units, with a variety of problems and perspectives. But of course it would not be enough blandly to state that there is always conflict; the fundamental implications are that management is the management of conflict and that the separate claims must somehow be reconciled with the need to hold the organization together, and with the global resources of the organization. In this situation, as in others discussed earlier, the 'political' aspect is most to the fore in ill-structured problems, those for which there do not exist easily programmed decisions. It should be noted, however, that even where there appear to be precise answers to problems, management may in practice be faced with ambiguity and uncertainty. Consider, for example, the mechanization of letter sorting offices in the postal business; it was perfectly possible to have detailed figures of likely cash flow and these were undoubtedly very helpful. But they were naturally based on assumptions about the future which could not be quite certain and some of which might be invalidated with the passage of time. Moreover, there were a number of interests to be considered and numbers of individuals involved in the decision process. This process included, therefore, the preparation of data and also the conduct of discussion and negotiation; there was a non-automaton management process.

How this process is conducted varies from organization to organization: it depends on many factors, among them being the personality characteristics and managerial style of the top executives or group of executives. Some organizations are more hierarchical than others, some more concerned with securing consensus. Much of the experience of the modern corporation does suggest, however, that political processes of negotiation, bargaining, trade-offs, and balancing of viewpoints and interests are widespread forms of business behaviour. These processes are formal and informal, regulated and *ad hoc*; as Bradley and Wilkie remark, 'The structure of an organization may . . . be viewed as a required pattern of behaviour.'[20] Understood and accepted ways of doing (or not doing) things are important, especially in areas of work which do not lend themselves readily to precise rules and regulations. Numbers of writers have drawn attention to the 'conventions of government', the working practices and relationships which grow up within an organization and form part of a constitution in terms of which the management functions. These conventions are found in a variety of institutions: Maddick and Pritchard wrote about them in the context of local government in the West Midlands in 1958–9, while more recently the term was applied in a study of a number of large business enterprises in Britain.[21] Lindblom's work and Quinn's writing on the management of the strategic process bring out the distinctive political dimension, formal and informal, of management activity.

CHAPTER EIGHT

STRATEGY AND PLANNING: WHAT HAS HAPPENED TO
THE CORPORATE PLANNERS?

The theme of strategy is now widely discussed in books on management and business policy, but perhaps the most appropriate starting-point is the pioneering work of Igor Ansoff in his book *Corporate Strategy*, which was published in 1965 and which he followed with a number of studies on the same theme. Another classic exposition is given by Kenneth Andrews in *The Concept of Corporate Strategy*, which first appeared in 1971.[1]

Why are the ideas of strategy and structure so important for management? There are three main reasons:

1. All writers on these themes, despite differences in the detail of their definitions, emphasize that strategy is concerned with those decisions which determine the direction which an enterprise is taking. The formulation of strategy is thus a primary determinant of the character of an organization.

2. There is a relationship between the strategy of an organization and its structure. The nature of this relationship, how strategy influences the way an enterprise is organized, how, in turn, the structure of an organization affects its strategy, are bound to affect the outlook and decisions of managers.

3. The view which is taken of how strategy is created and implemented, of who plays a part in making it, and of who carries responsibility for designing the organization, is a guideline to what is expected of managers – in other words, to the qualities which are necessary for good management at different levels.

The meaning of strategy

Many of the writers who define strategy are essentially concerned with the strategy of the enterprise as a whole. Ansoff approached the idea in the following way. Micro-economic theory, he said, had neglected the study of strategy because it had assumed that every business had one, known objective and had knowledge of all the relevant factors and outcomes. In reality, the *choice* of what strategy to pursue was the basic decision for any enterprise.

There are, said Ansoff, three categories of decision:

- strategic
- administrative
- operating

Expressed very simply, strategic decisions are concerned with what he termed the *product-market mix* or *scope* of the enterprise. By this he meant the products the firm sets out to supply, and the markets in which it seeks to supply them. In other words, business strategy is concerned with the question 'What kind of firm are we?' or, as other writers have put it, perhaps rather grandiosely, 'What is the strategic mission of the business?'[2] For example, Cadbury Schweppes would define the strategic scope of the company as the supply of snack foods, many of which happen to be chocolate-covered, through certain types of channel of distribution, notably supermarkets. Tarmac would see itself as a construction and civil engineering company. A previous chairman and chief executive of the company, R. G. Martin, discussing its policy on acquisitions, applied the idea of what he called 'compatibility' – though it seemed easier in fact to specify what he regarded as incompatible. Thus, he said, Tarmac would not seek to enter into businesses which required high skill in research and development or in consumer-durable goods (such as refrigerators or television sets), because the company was not equipped to handle the requirements of those areas. In other words, incompatibility could be translated as meaning: lying outside the strategic competence of the company.

These examples can be multiplied from both business and non-business sectors, and the initiation and development of organizations can perhaps be interpreted as a profile of the strategic choices which are made in them. Consider, for example, the changing pattern of Woolworth (referring to the company in Britain). It had grown into a chain of about one thousand stores occupying prime High Street sites and selling as variety stores at the low price end of the market. Some British readers, at least, will remember Woolworth as a 'three-penny' and 'sixpenny' store. More recently, in response to rising income levels in Britain and to changes in the competitive environment of the company, a deliberate strategy of up-marketing was introduced. Woolworth began to sell clothing, furniture, a range of foodstuffs, and other products aimed at a wider section of middle-income groups, and trying to shed the image of a cheap variety store.

This instance fits the idea of strategy as a matter of product-market scope: Woolworth was choosing its range of products and the kinds of market in which it proposed to sell. Mr Fung King Hey, a leading Hong Kong businessman, asked how he saw his company, replied that it sought to become 'an international financial and invest-ment superstore'. His strategy was to offer a range of financial facili-ties from which customers could 'pick up' their requirements in the same way that customers select what they want in a general super-market. Mr Fung's striking phrase encapsulated very neatly a state-ment of strategic choice.[3]

Kenneth Andrews defines the concept, in very broad terms, as follows:

Corporate strategy is the pattern of decisions in a company that determines and reveals its objectives, purposes, or goals, produces the principal policies and plans for achieving those goals, and defines the range of business the company is to pursue, the kind of economic organization it is or intends to be, and the nature of the economic and noneconomic contribution it intends to make to its shareholders, employees, customers and communities.[4]

Excessively broad though this definition must appear, it does offer a number of useful guidelines, and it is valuable for the study of management to view it in several contrasting ways. The first way is to assert that the management of enterprises does consciously choose a strategic direction and devise plans to carry it out. A second way is to say that managements frequently do *not* proactively manage the strategic process but that they *should* do so (and that they could do so, if only they would try). A third approach is to take the very first phrases of Andrews' definition and say that strategy (whether positively planned or not) is *revealed* in the decisions actually made. This is to envisage the pattern or flow of decisions as if it were like the path of a boat through the water, its direction revealed by the wake it leaves behind it.

Hofer and Schendel express similar points in this way:

> *The basic characteristic of the match an organization achieves with its environment is called its strategy.* The concept of strategy is thus one of top management's major tools for coping with both external and internal changes.
>
> Another aspect of the concept of strategy is that all organizations can be said to have a strategy. Thus, while the match between an organization's resources and its environment may or may not be explicitly developed and while it may or may not be a good match, the characteristics of this match can be described for all organizations.[5]

Thus, all these writers, Ansoff, Andrews, Hofer and Schendel, conceive of strategy as the problem of positioning the enterprise in relation to its external environment. They do not all view strategy in exactly the same way: indeed they do not all define it with the same attempted exactitude. The words 'goals', policies', 'objectives', 'strategies' are used in somewhat different ways. But all of these authors, and businessmen too, see corporate strategy as concerned with the direction of the enterprise – what kind of thing is it going to be doing? The strategic decisions which determine this direction, whether they are deliberate and proactive or responsive and reactive, are made necessary by the pressures and opportunities which are generated and afforded by the internal and external environments of the enterprise. It does not follow that every enterprise will make the decisions, but that strategic change *ought* to be recognized and that strategic decisions *should* be made.

Before examining these points in greater detail, something has to be said about strategy and non-business organizations. Andrews refers to 'a company', while Hofer and Schendel slip almost imperceptibly from the term 'organization' to 'firm'. It is possible, of course, to speak of strategy in a variety of organizations: in recent years, for example, universities in Britain and elsewhere have been giving closer, explicit attention to the question of which areas should receive higher priority than others. Even churches have given consideration to strategy in the sense of choosing sectors of the population on which to concentrate primary effort. It is easier to think of strategy in terms of business: the term comes more trippingly off the tongue when it can be envisaged in relation to products which have to be put to the test of the market. But strategic mission, in Professor Drucker's sense of the words, is not unique to business; other kinds of organization define their position in relation to an external environment.

Policy, strategy and the importance of strategic decisions

The usage of these words can be very confusing: for example, it is sometimes said that the study of business *policy* is concerned with the formation of business *strategy*. Andrews distinguishes between *corporate* strategy, by which he means the enterprise as a whole, and *business* strategies, by which he refers to the separate parts or businesses of which the total organization is composed. A government might say 'Our *policy* is to provide a specified level and quality of education for all young people.' But it might equally say 'Our *policy* is to improve the economic performance of the country, and a *strategy* we are adopting to achieve this is to increase the amount of educational provision.' Two other examples will illustrate this problem of language. Hofer and Schendel speak of corporate strategy as 'a tool for integrating an organization's diverse functional area policies', but they go on to give their own statement as follows: for the complex, multi-industry company, 'with multiple layers of general management hierarchy', they distinguish between corporate and business strategy. They reserve the first of those terms for the determination of the range of businesses in which the company should be active. This is akin to the idea of corporate strategic mission. They use the term business strategy to refer to the question: how should the corporation act in any of the particular businesses in which it is operating? The two constituents are not identical, but there is clearly a connection between them, and how to handle the relationship is, in fact, a significant part of management in complex companies.[6]

The important aspect for this chapter is the relationship between strategy and the tasks of management, and it will be useful, therefore, to set out how the various words are used here:

- POLICY is taken to refer to the general framework or set of values within which strategy is formulated. John Friend describes it as a 'stance', a general position which is taken up. The example cited earlier regarding employment in Rugby Portland Cement illustrates what is meant. A. S. Mackintosh, in his study of thirty-six firms, found that certain general attitudes dictated the strategies which could be considered by the firms.[7] Retention of family control, reluctance to borrow from certain kinds of lender, acted as policy *constraints* on strategic choice. Some strategies were not acceptable because they would have transgressed policy values which were dear to the companies. Those values are not immutable; they may change under the pressure of circumstances, but they are important as long as they stand.

- STRATEGY deals with the product-market pattern of the enterprise as a whole; Ansoff devotes much of his attention to diversification precisely because of its strategic importance in changing the range of products the firm supplies and the markets in which it supplies them. If a company comprises a number of subsidiaries or divisions, they may have strategies of their own, but in general these may be perceived as *sub-strategies* of the whole organization. It really depends on the perspective from which decisions are viewed. For example, in one large company, the managing director of a subsidiary which was, in itself, a large business, employing nearly ten per cent of the labour force of the entire group, said that he did not consider diversifying outside his established product range. He left that kind of decision to group headquarters. But he felt quite free to decide that his own company should diversify geographically by effecting major entry into the North American market. For him, this was a strategic decision; for the group, it could be regarded as a sub-strategy. The critical *management* question is not narrowly definitional: the question is, at what point does a decision take on strategic consequence for the whole corporation?

These separate decisions, group and divisional or subsidiary, are interrelated. What is done within one part of a business affects the whole; and corporate decisions for a whole group involve choices which govern the scope available to each part of it. But there is not always a crystal-clear distinction between them, and organizations may differ both in respect of what they feel are matters of strategic concern to the corporation as a whole and in the forms of strategic control which they employ. Or, again, some decisions are seen, in advance, to be of strategic consequence; but there are others which are seen to be so only with hindsight.

- GOALS and OBJECTIVES are often used interchangeably. Sometimes, however, a convenient, if not very precise, distinction is made between them. *Goals* refer to broad, general aims, for instance, to be the biggest company in a particular field, or as in Mr Fung King Hey's statement about creating a superstore of financial services. Examples of *objectives* might be to expand into overseas markets, or to increase market share at a desired rate; in other words, objectives specify the company's aims in operational terms. But the distinction is, perhaps, a tenuous one.

Why are strategic decisions important? First of all, the fact that they deal with the direction of the enterprise, its future size and pattern of outputs and markets, means that they determine the kind of company which has to be managed and the kinds of management talents which are called for. It used to be thought that management was something universal and that any manager could handle any kind of organization, especially in the higher reaches of management which do not call for specific, functional skills. As a matter of fact, this view has greatly influenced the development of management education, and, as the argument of Chapter 2 on the generalist character of management has suggested, it holds a large kernel of truth. On the other hand, the strategic choices in an enterprise establish, over a period of time, a pattern of outlooks and skills, a knowledge of 'the fine structure of production' in defined fields of activity, and, as Professor Penrose has emphasized, a management team, whose members together establish the *distinctive competence* or *personality* of an organization.[8]

Secondly, and relatedly, the formulation of strategy, *insofar as it is consciously considered and planned*, actually *obliges* an enterprise to consider what it is trying to achieve. What are its objectives, how shall it expand, what, if any, diversification is appropriate? Hence the broad strategic decisions of an enterprise lead to a cascade of other managerial decisions. When a company decides to expand substantially, or to diversify its product lines, or to enter new markets overseas, there will be consequences in terms of capital expenditure, the allocation of resources between separate parts of the company, changes in structure and marketing practices, and in personnel requirements.

Thirdly, there are significant relationships between the strategy to which an organization is wedded and the structural form it adopts. What form those relationships may take is the subject of a later section in this chapter, but that they do exist is intuitively obvious. There will be some connection between, say, the variety of product lines a company provides and the way the company is organized: the establishment of product-based divisions is a possible instance. The link between strategy and structure is not the only one in a company, but it is clearly an important one. For example, when Woolworth in the UK adopted the up-market strategy referred to earlier, they were faced with the need to create new divisions in the company to cope with the new types of product with which they were now concerned. Even the type of leadership or direction may be affected: the managing director of one large company operating in a range of commodities in about forty countries remarked that they now had as chairman a man whose career had been in diplomacy. His experience was thought to be very appropriate to a company whose product range had expanded in countries where governments played a large part in economic affairs.

Lastly, strategic decisions are important because of the need they create for managers capable of making them in various layers of an organization. The strategies of growth, and of growth with diversification, have generated this need and increased the numbers of professional managers. The organizational aspects discussed in the following section underline this aspect.

The making of strategic decisions

In the modern corporation, as in smaller enterprises, the determination of corporate strategy is a critical function of the top management or direction of a company. It could hardly be otherwise, because if top management does not ultimately control the strategic path of a business – and the same goes for non-business organizations – how can it really be regarded as top management? Both the general policy values and the strategic choices have to lie with the individuals at the top, since otherwise they cannot be said to be at the top, or at best are figureheads. Recent studies of major companies have tended to demonstrate the importance of the most senior people in them, to the extent of suggesting that they are the repository and embodiment of entrepreneurship, even in very large business bureaucracies. They themselves seemed to be conscious of this: when John Neville spoke of the centre as leading the subsidiaries 'on the path of business discovery', he was referring to group headquarters in his company. But he undoubtedly meant himself as chief executive and his chairman Mr Poore – who took the same view. In the case of Thomas Tilling, a diversified group which regarded itself as the pioneer of the industrial holding company in Britain, the managing director of one of its major subsidiaries explicitly identified Sir Patrick Meaney, chief executive of the group, as the top man or entrepreneur. In Tarmac, the chairman Eric Pountain, and his senior colleagues at headquarters in Wolverhampton, saw themselves as responsible for setting the general pattern of the group, even though a high degree of autonomy was given to the separate divisions in the company. The long-term strategic direction was seen as their responsibility within a framework of the way they envisaged the company.

This is entirely in line with Ansoff's emphasis that strategic decisions tend to be centralized. There is another reason for this, reflected in Sir Adrian Cadbury's comment that only top management in a business corporation is able to take 'a wide enough view'. Only from the vantagepoint of the top of the mountain can the widest extent of the countryside be surveyed. Interestingly enough, one of the senior managers at the head of one of the divisions of Cadbury Schweppes made much the same point while looking at the matter from below the peak. He remarked that no head of a division will be disposed to recommend the contraction (not to say elimination or divestment) of his own division; it is, after all, hardly the way he is likely to think of his job. But decisions of that kind may have to be made; it is clear that they can only be made at a point which stands above the individual units. Just as the managers of individual functional departments cannot make decisions for the whole company solely in terms of their own functions, so it is that managing directors of divisions or subsidiaries in complex corporations cannot make decisions for the whole group in terms only of their own entities.

This also has a bearing on leadership in an organization, for it requires the ability to see the separate, internal parts as a whole, and to see the organization in relation to the external world which it inhabits. Pountain, chairman of Tarmac, emphasized the contribution made by the company as a group to the divisions in this regard, referring to its ability to talk to relevant interests outside the company. He clearly saw this as something the top direction could provide. Again, a crucial characteristic of general management – and strategy is the most general form that management can take – is the capacity to conceptualize, i.e. to frame a general idea or picture of the purpose of the enterprise as a whole. Andrews adds that it requires, also, 'the dramatic skill to invest it with some degree of magnetism.'[9] This is sometimes reflected too in the impact of a new chief executive whose arrival provides a focus for significant changes in strategic direction and emphasis in a company.

So far, it might be thought, all this is straightforward, and even painfully obvious. Strategic decisions are the most important of all decisions; top management holds ultimate responsibility for deciding where the enterprise is going, and hence has responsibility for strategy. Other managers are implementers of strategy and will be more concerned with the operational decisions which derive from carrying out strategy. But is this really so? Is it possible to divide up strategy formulation and implementation so tidily, and is this feasible even in the large, divisionalized modern business enterprise? The question is important, not only as a matter of academic interest, but also to management, since on the answer to it will depend what is to be expected of managers at various levels, and how they should be developed and trained. Another, connected aspect arises; strategic change is typically associated with the idea of entrepreneurship since both terms are taken to refer to selecting fresh directions – moving into new product and market patterns. Where, then, is entrepreneurship to be identified in the modern corporation? Is it in one place, is it with one person, or is it more widely dispersed throughout the company?

The first part of any answer to these questions is itself a question. Where do ideas come from in any organization? Any significant strategic departure in an enterprise depends initially on an idea or set of ideas; the British economist Shackle speaks of entrepreneurial activity as something creative, every act of choice representing a new beginning. Imagination as well as reason is a key to understanding business decision. Or, again, how does the need for strategic change make itself felt?

Clearly, there are moments of imaginative impulse, the recognition or creation of business opportunities, whether these are associated with individual names, like Laura Ashley or Mary Quant or Terence Conran of Habitat, or with the apparently anonymous modern corporation. But the development of strategy, especially in the corporation, is in more than one moment in time; as Quinn says, it is a 'long evolution'. Moreover, even when it can be said that a strategy has been adopted, this is not the end of the management task, since what the enterprise is doing will have to be reassessed in the context of a changing environment. Writing of the experience of one of the companies he studied, Quinn says that 'skilled executives carefully arranged to have new people constantly moving into the decision stream and challenging past assumptions with new ideas and potentials.'[10]

Numbers of industrialists, in discussing the origins of strategic change in their companies, have emphasized the plurality of sources of ideas in a company. Neville and Cadbury spoke of a triangle or pyramid within which ideas occurred in various parts, the question being how to pull out those ideas and to bring them to the point where they might form part of the strategy of the company. The point was made earlier that only from the top could a wide enough view be taken; but it is also true, so a number of top managers have said, that the headquarters of an enterprise could hardly be expected, of itself, to be aware of all the possible directions of change via, say, diversification.

These comments are quite general; there are also a number of specific factors which emphasize the part played by various levels of management in the formation of corporate strategy. One of these is inherent in the nature of information flow within an organization. Even though the fundamental responsibility for determining corporate strategy is vested in the top – and it is there that it must, at all events, be approved and authorized – much of the information on which decisions are based must come from other levels of management. In other words, the way top management sees the world is partly governed by information which has been prepared by, say, middle managers. This information has necessarily been summarized and filtered; it includes what lower levels of management consider to be important and it will reflect their biases, functional and other kinds. This aspect must not be exaggerated; strong-minded chief executives are perfectly capable of looking for themselves or of asking for new information and fresh options. In fact, one of the striking characteristics of such executives appears to be their command of detail; they do not sit solitary at their desks and behave as brooding overlords. Nevertheless, they do have to depend on information from subordinates and to be able to repose trust in them. The balance of these considerations is summed up by Alford in his analysis of the two-way relationship between the strategy of an enterprise and its organizational structure. He pointed to the influence which managers can exert on a company's strategic decisions in their capacity as generators and regulators of information within it. At the same time, good top executives know what kind of information to ask for and how to ask for it: this is one mark of a good executive. In other words, managers below the top do not have unlimited licence to determine the perceptions of their senior people.

But, as Alford goes on to point out, business policies (here meaning strategic direction) are based on accumulated information built up through time, much of it generated in the ongoing operations of the divisional units which constitute the corporation.[11]

This is one feature which suggests that the formulation of strategy is more complex than a simple picture of top strategy makers/lower-level strategy implementers and that 'what may be termed "diffused entrepreneurship" is almost certainly a widespread feature of large managerial companies.' Another specific feature is particularly well brought out by Bower in a consideration of the planning process in business. He points out that while top management is concerned with 'the overall relationship of the company to its environment' (which is equivalent to Ansoff's concept of strategy),

Middle levels of management face the difficult task of reconciling the multiple product-market plans of sub-units with each other and with top management plans for the face of the company in the global environment.

But, he goes on to say,

where complexity or diversity keep top management from comprehending the substance of their businesses, plans and capital projects are initiated at sub-unit levels. Top management focuses on broad questions they perceive to be critical.[12]

If this is so, then the direction of a corporation will be influenced by an accumulation of planning decisions and projects which have originated in the operating divisions or subsidiaries of a group. Decisions which are taken in this way and at these levels may have significant consequences for an organization: in this sense, they become part of its strategy. Moreover, the whole phenomenon of 'diffused entrepreneurship' is probably more striking now than at any time, because the development of technological and other kinds of expertise has tended to create situations in which special knowledge and 'technical imperatives' play a predetermining part.

A great deal has been written in the past two decades on strategy as an organizational process, and much research is in progress. There are large gaps in knowledge about the relationship between the influence of the top personality or dominant figure and the organizational processes necessarily involved in the large managerial complexes which are so prevalent. The evidence which research has brought forward so far, however, does suggest on the one hand that the entrepreneur is not yet dead, and on the other, that 'strategic choice is not merely the function of the chief executive office.' One implication of this proposition is that a capacity to think strategically is not a requirement solely of top management. Another implication is that the management of large organizations calls for control of the strategic process, not only at the top, but throughout the system.[13]

Strategy and organization

Kenneth Arrow wrote in 1964 that 'Truly among man's innovations, the use of organization to accomplish his ends is among his greatest and earliest.'[14]

Many of the things that people wish to do can be accomplished only by creating an organization, for, again as Arrow points out, organizations reflect the fact that many tasks require the participation of numbers of individuals. Decisions are just the same: they also often require the contribution of different persons with a variety of knowledge and skills. In this section, therefore, the link between strategy and organizational form comes under consideration, particularly in the context of the two fundamental strategies of growth and diversification.

Consider, first of all, a very simple schema, the development of a business from a one-man or one-woman beginning. In this case, all the business functions have to be carried out by one person; if, however, there is a relative or partner who shares the work of the business, it is likely that some division of labour will occur. One person will perhaps concentrate on selling, the other on buying in stock. As the business expands, three problems may arise: the volume of work will become too much for one person alone, the variety of skills will be too many, and the geographical spread too wide. The extent to which hardworking founders of businesses can cope with growth is, in fact, often quite remarkable; but at some stage the principle of managerial overload is bound to apply. Some of the difficulties can be overcome by using the services of external personnel (accountants, consultants) and, as activity increases, by the full-time employment of such personnel. Ultimately, however, the sheer growth in scale gives rise to the development of departmentalization in a rudimentary or sophisticated form. Thus, for example:

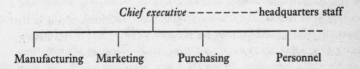

This form of organization, known as functional or U-form (i.e. unitary), would come about because the growth of the business, whether by conscious strategic design or unconscious strategic response, had created the need for delegation and decentralization in management. And it means that there has been some delegation of decision-making authority within the overall control of the chief executive or board of directors. This clearly helps to resolve some of the problems of overload; but it will not resolve them all. Thus, if there is conflict between the departments which it proves impossible to solve at inter-departmental level, problems will float up to the top – which will become over-burdened once again. That is why a head-quarters staff may be valuable, a staff, moreover, providing the chief executive with specialist advice free of departmental bias.

Suppose now a situation in which a company diversifies its product line – that it has engaged in a strategy of growth and diversification. Top management is now faced with the questions which stimulated departmentalization plus the difficulty of comprehending a range of products which may have different characteristics in technology, markets, and personnel. How might management cope with this situation? A characteristic method would is shown in the diagram opposite.

In this example, the divisions are often based on products: this form of divisionalized structure is known as the M-form (multi-divisional). It has also been described as 'federal decentralization', and this phrase is especially apt because it brings out the managerial aspects and exemplifies those problems of control which were first raised in the previous chapter. Each division is almost a company – a quasi-firm, it has been said – very often with a high degree of autonomy. In fact, John Neville spoke of the requirement in the Manganese Bronze Group for the managing directors of its subordinate companies to run their companies as businesses – rather, it might be said, as if they were running their own businesses. The significance of the M-form, from a management point of view, is that it transfers decision-making to divisions which are close to the products with which they are concerned. In addition, it provides opportunity for general managers (as well as those operating within specific functions) who can run a business. Of course, it also creates a need for such managers. Frank T. Cary, who was chief executive

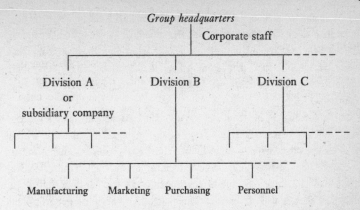

officer and chairman of the board of International Business Machines Corporation and who continued as chairman of the executive committee of the IBM board of directors, described in 1985 the use of Independent Business Units (IBU) in the corporation. These were small groups with the responsibility for managing a whole business area, such as robotic systems, running it as a small company with its own directors. They were intended to help in the better management of the whole business, but they also served to provide some individuals with an opportunity to acquire wider management experience early on.[15]

This brief outline of two possible organizational forms suggests a link between strategy and structure. In the concluding paragraphs of his book of that title, Chandler emphasizes the link between them and with 'the changing nature of the market'. The extent to which companies have adopted a multi-divisional structure, or something akin to it, is a matter of historical record. It is also clear that companies may adopt a particular structure in close response to strategic change. Hugh Norton, at British Petroleum, relates organizational change in the company during the 1970s to the deliberate strategy of diversification which was prompted by its assessment of the changing conditions in the oil industry. The company was concerned to combine, in matrix form, the organizational requirements imposed by an increase in product lines, with its commitments as a multi-national company. It did so by an arrangement which provided for a product organization which was worldwide, with a country-based organization in such a way that, for example, there would be an overall unit or division for a particular product group wherever that product was made or supplied; at the same time, the head of, say, Australian operations would be responsible for all BP products handled in that country.

In this instance, Norton was saying that structure follows strategy, that the task of management is to devise organizational form which enables the enterprise to meet its management problems and to attain its purposes. This is again like the point made by Chandler in his studies of the development of corporations in the United States; he observes that it was diversification in product scope or geographical areas which usually prompted the rise of the multi-divisional form. It came in response to management problems to which the functional form of organization was not well adapted.[16] In Britain, he says, the M-form came considerably later, because of the different historical development of the two countries: but come it has done, when he claims that 'the days of family and personal management were numbered', after the war.

But this is not the whole of the story, for just as indeed strategy may influence structure, so may the reverse be true; the way an enterprise is organized may influence the strategies it adopts. In any organizational structure, individuals and departments have been assigned responsibilities to carry out tasks, and experience suggests that tasks are only likely to be carried out if those responsibilities have been allocated. If it is nobody's business to do something, if no unit exists which is required to deal with particular tasks, then it is unlikely that the relevant questions will be asked or the relevant opportunities perceived. The creation of an organizational structure is a means of focusing attention on problems and prospects. It is also the system of channels through which information is directed, and in this way it influences the picture of the environment which is seen by top management.

A further element is that organization represents stability; people know (or should know) where they are, who is responsible for what, and who is accountable to whom. Strategic change may be very disturbing; it may change the organizational requirements and the authority influence and status of departments and individuals. Some of the things which managers have learned have to be unlearned, and fresh ideas and practices have to be absorbed. Change is not only disturbing; it involves costs in resources, readjustment and fresh learning. There may thus be some tendency for organizations to limit the strategies they are prepared to consider to those which can be handled within the existing framework or with only modest adjustments to it. Other strategies will perhaps not be seriously considered because of the costs and disturbance to which they may give rise.

How far these factors are significant, how great is the part they play, are questions which can only be answered by careful study. But there is good reason to believe that they do count, and to the extent that they do, it will be organization that governs strategy as much as the other way round. More appropriately, it may be said that there is a two-way interplay between them.

The consequence of this idea for management and managers is that the design of organizational structure is so closely allied to the strategic process that it can be regarded as a part of it. The formulation of strategy is inseparable from the creation of the corporate and business structures required to make it effective.

How does strategy emerge?

It will be evident from the preceding sections that the formulation of strategy in any complex organization is itself a complex process. It is, so to speak, a multi-dimensional landscape rather than a hierarchical picture of instructions from the top, compliance from below. Hierarchy and authority certainly count, and so does the dynamism and influence of the top individual. Indeed, the success of many businesses can be closely related to the character and drive of one man or woman, or a small group. But these factors do not count for everything; moreover, the ability of dominant individuals lies partly in their understanding of the processes of organization, of how, as Cadbury and Neville put it, to draw ideas from all parts of the enterprise so that they can be translated into marketable and profitable opportunities. Even the Midlands industrialist Crabtree, with his character both entrepreneurial and paternalistic, his insistence that

'In no case should the power of final decision on strategical issues be delegated', his warning against 'exaggerating the importance of organisations and system', and his belief that 'every industrial combine tends to crystallise round the catalyst of a single personality', nevertheless emphasizes

that periodically one has at times to review the whole business in its fundamentals, and without prejudice by any existing organisation, decide what organisation is necessary to cope with the business for the immediate future.[17]

Crabtree was making these comments in the context of a company of modest size; he was describing organizational and leadership problems in terms of a few hundred employees (at maximum one thousand). It must be still more the case in very large and complex enterprises that the strategic pattern is formed by numbers of contributors. If this is so, then the *management* of the strategic process is a really critical feature in a modern business. It will not be simply a matter of a top management which devises strategy and which then has to ensure that it is implemented; the process includes drawing in ideas and securing effective commitment.

Many writers on management and many textbooks emphasize the importance of planning the strategy of an enterprise. One of the leading American writers, Peter Drucker, attaches special significance to defining the 'strategic mission' of the company; and books of business policy case studies used for teaching in universities and colleges focus on the rational, planned steps which should be followed in diagnosing a business case. Specifying goals and objectives, environmental analysis, diagnosing company strengths and weaknesses, are characteristic phrases with which students become familiar. Corporate planning and corporate planners have come to the fore in recent decades; the Strategic Management Society, with its international membership of academics and business executives and its *Strategic Management Journal*, has flourished. A good deal of work has been done which attempts to compare the performance of companies which have formal planning systems with those which have not. The study of strategic management and planning has found a place in non-business as well as business institutions. And yet, coincident with the rise of corporate planners, there is said to have been disenchantment with them (see Chapter 9 below). There is a discrepancy between the emphasis which writers like Ansoff, Andrews, Hofer and Schendel place on strategic planning and the political process which is reflected in some of the writing discussed earlier in Chapter 4. Quinn puts it in the following way. He had started, in the late 1950s and early 1960s, from the opinion that better decision-making would occur in large organizations if they had good, more rational planning systems. But then he noted what he calls 'three disturbing tendencies'.

These were: the tendency for planning to become inflexible, to be a 'costly paper-shuffling exercise', the observed phenomenon that even in large enterprises the major strategic decisions were mostly made outside the planning framework, and, perhaps most disturbing of all from the present point of view, the discrepancy between the sophisticated models in the management literature and the way in which systems actually work. In these circumstances, formal planning was liable to be 'just another aspect of controllership – and another weapon in organizational politics'. That strategy should arise outside a planning framework in the case of smaller enterprises is perhaps unsurprising but that this should also be so in large corporations, with established habits and structures of formal planning, is a striking comment on the true sources of strategic ideas.[18]

More detailed examination of the function of planning is undertaken in the following chapter. But several points may be re-emphasized here. Quinn is saying that formal planning structures are no substitute for strategic creativity; indeed the bureaucracy and rigidity they engender tend to be inimical to it. In fact, it is not through the formal processes that strategy is created, especially in smaller enterprises, but also in large ones. Finally, his remarks about the 'sophisticated models' mean that they are neither descriptive of real processes, i.e. the ways in which organizations actually work, nor desirable methods for dealing with strategy, i.e. they do not offer helpful prescriptions.

Does this mean that management and managers should not be interested in planning at the strategic level in their companies? Does it mean that managers should not be themselves equipped, or utilize the services of staff who have been equipped, with methodologies and techniques which have been extensively developed? This is certainly not the case, nor do Quinn and other writers like him suggest it, and for two very good reasons. Firstly, a planning procedure allows managers to examine the future of a company in a systematic fashion and to utilize quantitative and other data as indicators of possible costs and benefits of different courses of action. Focusing attention in this way is especially important because, as has been pointed out, there is a powerful tendency for managers to concentrate on operating decisions, and, at the same time, 'excessive attention to the operating decisions may well cause organizations to do the incorrect things more efficiently.' Secondly, ideas of strategic interest may emerge *during* the planning process, as spin-offs from the process. There are many enterprises which do have long-term plans and in which the numerical information as well as the general ideas are scrutinized very carefully. There are others in which there is profound scepticism about what has been called 'number crunching'; as the chief executive and his senior colleagues at Tarmac expressed it, the inaccuracy of the targets destroyed their credibility. Since they never hit those (long-term) targets 'by a mile', nobody believed in them. The critical points, however, are these:

1. The fact that there may be no explicit long-term plan does not mean that there is no strategic thinking about the direction a company is taking. It may be discussed formally or, as can be the case, informally, on a continuing basis. The same executives who were so scathing about 'number crunching' pointed out that they themselves worked together very closely. They meant this quite literally: they had neighbouring offices and met and 'talked shop' about the company a great deal.

2. In some cases, perhaps in many, companies give explicit consideration to definition of strategic mission, to positioning themselves in the market in the context of general stated aims (*policies* in the language of this chapter). But even if they do not, strategic decisions *are* made, and they may be made as part and parcel of the ongoing problems and opportunities which constitute business experience. Sometimes, looking back on business decisions, it may seem as if

there was a well-considered, meticulously worked-out grand design. But looking forward, it may well have been much more like a series of continuing responses and stages of action provoked by the succession of problems posed to a firm in its efforts to ensure its effective survival.

3. Strategy may evolve through time, incrementally, even where there are formal planning systems, and may be implemented in trial stages, as when a company experiments, say, with test selling in a geographical segment of a national market before extending the sales effort to the whole country.

Quinn argues that

The most effective strategies of major enterprises tend to emerge step by step from an iterative process in which the organization probes the future, experiments, and learns from a series of partial (incremental) commitments rather than through global formulations of total strategies. *Good managers are aware of this process, and they consciously intervene in it. They use it to improve the information available for decisions and to build the psychological identification essential to successful strategies. The process is both logical and incremental.*[19] [Italics added]

4. Extending that argument, Quinn makes it clear that his view is entirely compatible with the existence of global aims. What he insists on is that there is no one perfect model, that the process by which strategies emerge is 'logical and incremental', and that it is actively utilized and managed by good managers. Obviously there are commitments with long-term horizons and consequences, for example major investment projects in electricity or communications. It is the management process, how it is handled, which is what Quinn has particularly in mind.

It can be seen how closely this view of the strategic process fits into the idea of organizational management as a 'political' activity, and of organizations as systems of governance with both formal structures and informal processes. Sometimes, of course, major crises, in, say, market conditions faced by the firm, may overwhelm the incremental process, or a major breakthrough may shift the parameters of action. But there is wider evidence that good management in strategic decisions characteristically involves, at least in the larger business corporation, 'continuous evolving political consensus – building processes with no precise beginning or end.'[20] The analysis here is in the same dimension as the general argument of Chapter 4, where it was emphasized by Lindblom that the skilful practitioner of 'muddling through' is not muddled, nor is the incrementalist disjointed. A consensus in decision-making leading to business action develops over a period of time. The process has to be managed, and good managers need to know how to do it, using ideas and techniques of different kinds.

How things will actually work out will depend on a variety of considerations, such as the nature of the decisions required, the kind of organization involved (e.g. business or public administration), cultural differences (e.g. in attitudes towards hierarchy), size of organization, managerial style and the power of individual personalities. But the essence of the matter is that strategic decisions are not simply isolated moments in time but are part of the continuing life of the organization. They involve complex processes of generation, development and acceptance at more than one level of management, and they impose a requirement for strategic thinking capacity at more than one level.

CHAPTER NINE

PLANNING IN THE BUSINESS CORPORATION

Planning is widely perceived as a characteristic function of management, and the idea and the methods are extensively discussed in the literature. What is a plan, and how should it be constructed? Who should do the planning in a company, and what kinds of plan are desirable? Is planning worthwhile: does it improve company performance? Even the definition of the word can present some difficulties or ambiguities. Peter Hall, for example, in his book *Great Planning Disasters*, points to two meanings: one refers to 'a set of *processes* whereby decision-makers engage in logical foresight before committing themselves'; the other refers to 'processes that result in a *physical plan* showing the distribution of activities and their related structures (houses, factories, offices, schools) in geographical space.'[1] Ackoff speaks of planning as 'the design of a desired future and of effective ways of bringing it about.'[2] Lorange and Vancil, in discussing strategic planning, say that 'A strategic planning system is nothing more than a structured (that is, designed) process that organizes and coordinates the activities of the managers who do the planning.'[3]

This chapter is primarily concerned with the 'logical foresight' and 'co-ordination' definitions (of which, of course, the outcome may be the physical plan); it is concerned both with the corporate level of strategic plans and the more specific plans at the operational levels of an enterprise.

The firm as a planning system

Any individual may seek to exercise logical foresight, to think ahead, and to design his future. In this sense, individuals and families undertake an activity which may be called 'planning'. The key words for them, as for an organization, are foresight and co-ordination; planning means anticipation of future events, the design of a desired outcome, and the co-ordination of multiple decisions. This may apply in the comparatively simple case of planning a future holiday, or the more complicated case of career planning. The eponymous hero of H. G. Wells's novel *Love and Mr Lewisham* had designed a whole chart to map out the stages of his prospective career (a plan which was rendered obsolete by his early marriage).

To think ahead and to effect co-ordination are not, however, quite the same thing as planning. A consumer may think he wishes to go to buy a product or may buy it on impulse from a shopkeeper or a street trader. The buyer and seller are brought together by the market, through the operation of the price mechanism. This is a wholly decentralized form of co-ordination. In a famous article published in 1937, 'The Nature of the Firm', R. H. Coase contrasted this form of co-ordination through the price mechanism with co-ordination within the boundaries of the firm.[4] The essence of his analysis was that he saw the firm as something which replaced the unconscious co-ordination effected by price signals with conscious, managerial co-ordination. Instead of an invisible hand, in Adam Smith's immortal phrase, the visible hand of management is to be seen: Coase referred to an 'entrepreneur-coordinator' in a firm; Chandler entitled his book on the rise of industrial enterprise in the United States *The Visible Hand*. Arrow says the same kind of thing: 'A firm, especially a large corporation, provides another major area within which price relations are held in partial abeyance.'[5] In the quotation given on p. 107, using the example of the automobile engine division, March and Simon observe that transactions within organizations differ from market transactions in that they are far more a matter of pre-planning and pre-co-ordination. The structure of an organization and its procedures are means of co-ordinating the separate plans of the separate departments and divisions within it.

These general definitions and statements are made in order to emphasize that the very existence of a business firm is a statement about a form of planning. When Coase writes about the firm as taking over from the price mechanism, and Arrow writes of holding price relations suspended, they are in effect making the same point as March and Simon. Co-ordination in the firm is brought about by managers and managerial decision-making. The firm is an area of planning. Consider, for example, the decision whether to 'make or buy'; should the firm manufacture a required component itself or buy it in from a supplier in the market? If it buys it, the transaction is an *external* one; if it makes the component itself, then the decision process and the resultant activity are *internalized*: the boundaries of the firm have been extended. Or imagine a market with separate stallholders each paying a rent to the landlord who owns the property – something which can be seen in a number of towns and cities. What is the difference between this situation and the modern department store in the ownership of a single company? In the first instance, the stallholder decides what to sell, what stock to carry, and so on; in the latter, the central management makes or authorizes those decisions and is responsible, for example, for co-ordinating purchases and sales.

This is not the whole of the story of planning; it is focused primarily on the element of co-ordination. But it stresses that the distinction between market process and the internal decisions in firms is, in principle, a matter of *how* co-ordination is effected. In the sense delineated here, managers are inevitably involved in some element of planning, though it may be informal as well as formal. The case made here is not at all the same as saying that all firms have formal planning systems or even that they plan very much at all in the sense of having written plans. 'Formality', a senior industrialist remarked, 'is a function of size', and so, to some extent, is this likely to be true of detailed documentation of planning.[6] But the quotation from March and Simon is a valid statement of what it is that characterizes firms – pre-planning and pre-co-ordination.

A closer look at definitions

So far, planning has been considered in general terms, and in those terms most individuals and most organizations are likely to engage in at least a minimal amount of planning. Moreover, because individuals are likely to have goals, purposes they would like to fulfil, and because resources are limited, both they and the organizations of which they are members may have to make plans in order to try to match those goals and resources. In the picture painted so far, it could be said that the very existence of organizations means that there has been some centralization of the decision process, because decisions have been transferred from the decentralized mode of the price mechanism to the planning mode of managerial decision-making.

When people speak of planning in the business corporation, however, or in any other kind of organization, they usually mean something more than this; they have in mind a set of deliberate processes and procedures whose outcome is a set of general and specific plans which, it is hoped, will shape the future pattern of the organization. In a book of readings entitled *Long-Range Planning for Management*, the opening part is prefaced by three quotations; a philosophic one from Will Rogers: 'Even if you're on the right track, you'll get run over if you just sit there'; and another from Thomas Tusser: 'Look ere thou leap, see ere thou go.' These two statements encapsulate important principles, and they are underlined by the third, quoting Kierkegaard: 'Life can only be understood backwards, but must be lived forwards.'[7]

What are the principles, and how do they relate to management and planning? The first is that recognition of correct direction is not sufficient; positive decisions, i.e. commitments to a course of action, are required, which means thinking about how to get from point A to point B. The second is that foresight is called for when such commitments are taken into an uncertain future. The last point is of peculiar significance and it complements the discussion of decision-making in general and Drucker's insistence that 'Long range planning does not deal with future decisions. It deals with the futurity of present decisions.' Planning is concerned, not with future decisions, but with the impact of decisions which have to be made now and which will have consequences in the future. And however tidy the results may look with hindsight, plans are made at a time when the future is yet to come and the consequences can only be estimated. It is precisely for this reason that a case for planning can be made; it is because of the existence of risk and uncertainty in the real world that there is a case for systematic appraisal of problems and opportunities in a company and for attempts to match company resources with opportunities.

It is possible, therefore, to refine the definitions of planning more closely. To begin with, it can be said that:

- planning is an attempt systematically to match resources with opportunities
- in order to achieve specified purposes of the organization

This makes explicit that planning assumes that organizations have objectives which can be expressed in such a way that plans can be designed so as to achieve them, and that success in achieving them can be measured, either quantitatively or by other criteria which are meaningful and consistent.

- planning is the process or processes by which plans are formulated
- the plans express the decisions which are required to bring about the desired outcomes
- and the decisions are *anticipatory*, i.e. made now with respect to an as yet non-existent state

One writer has emphasized process by quoting President Eisenhower: 'Plans are nothing. Planning is everything.'[8] The point is that whereas any plan may be a final, or more or less final, document, the planning process is continuous, since both the internal and external environments may be changing and fresh plans may be required to respond to changing circumstances and possibilities.

- since planning is concerned with aligning objectives, resources and opportunities, it impinges on all those who are involved in the tasks of alignment, in other words, on managers. Planning is not purely a process for professional planners; it is an integral part of management
- in an organization, there are multiple objectives. Hence the planning process includes, not only the devising of plans aiming to attain objectives;

it also includes selection of objectives and the priorities which are accorded to them.

Writing in 1965 and seeing what he thought was 'the growing acceptance of formal planning', Ansoff stated that in the management of the business firm of the future 'Planning will be institutionalized, and the accounting, information, and control systems will be oriented toward future prospects, rather than past results.'[9] This view was indicative of emphasis on strategic management and on the need to give systematic attention to the long-run interests of the enterprise.

These statements about planning are essentially concerned with strategic planning, especially at the corporate level, i.e. planning which determines the main direction of the organization in products and markets. They also refer to how the organization itself is planned, since, as has already been pointed out, the development of strategy and the construction of organization are closely interrelated. The assumptions which underlie formal planning at the corporate level are that corporate goals can be clearly articulated, that the limits within which the enterprise is to operate can be fairly clearly defined, that strategy can be sufficiently flexible to cope with the unforeseeable course of events which may impinge on the chosen strategy, and that the separate plans of the units can be integrated into a corporate whole.

Put like this, corporate planning must seem a very tall order, and so it is. In his book *Corporate Governance*, Tricker refers to the idea of corporate complexity: studies by the Corporate Policy Group at Oxford, on which his book is based, included a project to develop data on the complex structure of corporations in the United Kingdom. For although complexity is emphasized in studies of management organizations, Tricker observes that 'there is no readily available measure of corporate complexity.'

A little later, in discussing 'the dispersion of power in complex groups', he goes on to say:

In a large public company, with many subsidiaries and divisions, operating in various businesses, in different parts of the world, power is likely to be exercised in various roles and at various levels. Understanding corporate governance is not just a matter of determining whether the main board or the members exercise power. It involves appreciating the roles and responsibilities of directors of subsidiary companies, managers of divisional businesses, and head office staff.[10]

In making those obervations, Tricker was particularly concerned with the questions: how do corporations actually function, how are they governed, and how does the legal definition of a corporation correspond (or fail to correspond) with the reality of corporate processes? He replies to his questions by outlining and elucidating the complexity of the modern corporation, composed, as it commonly is, of very large numbers of subsidiary companies with many levels of control. Tricker's analysis also has a bearing, however, on the meaning of corporate planning, because it raises the question: what, in reality, is meant by a business corporation? From the point of view of planning, the picture of complexity means that

- at the *top level* of the corporation, planning implies thinking about broad guidelines for policy or strategy. Adrian Cadbury drew attention to this in his view that top management should (could only) give a few guidelines to the senior managers in the group. He also referred to having a planning group in which the members could 'kick ideas around'.
- even at the top level, however, the formulation of the planning framework cannot really be made independently of the contribution of the subsidiary parts of the group. It could hardly be effective, especially in large companies: it has been pointed out in a number of studies of business that detailed knowledge of each part of a diversified corporation is primarily to be found in its divisions. That is where specialized knowledge of the particular product line, its customers, market conditions and management problems is located and where plans have to be formulated and implemented. Hence, while top management undoubtedly has a leadership role, it also has to count on the capacity of the divisions to run as businesses, to be sources of ideas, and to contribute their autonomous share in the corporate planning process.[11]
- because planning for the corporation is thus inseparable from the plans of the sub-units, even the corporate plan is not unequivocally a staff function at headquarters. It is also a line management activity at more than one level of the organization.

Planning, tidiness and system

One of the special problems which arises in discussions of planning, as with strategy and tactics, is that the words have connotations in military (and, perhaps, political) contexts and that it can be very confusing if they are translated without qualification into the field of business enterprise. Even in those contexts, clarity of objectives may be difficult to specify, and interactive relationships difficult to sustain; but in a business the authority and power relationships are likely to be somewhat different in character and intensity.

It is useful, therefore, to look at the concept of corporate planning in terms of precision and imprecision, and a good way is to consider Ackoff's exposition, based on what he called 'the systems revolution'. Any organization can be conceived as a *system*, by which is meant that

FIGURE FIVE

INTERACTIVE PLANNING

Principles	Content
1. PARTICIPATION: because the main benefit of planning comes from taking part in it	1. The 'mess' should be formulated, i.e. the problems and prospects identified
2. CONTINUITY: because plans have to be continuously revised in the light of future experience	2. Means-end planning should deal with the design of the desired future state
3. HOLISTIC: because (a) at each level of the organization, planning should be simultaneous and interdependent for all units, and because (b) each level should be planned interdependently to allow for the fact that levels are interrelated	3. Resource planning has to deal with the human, material, and information resources required
	4. Organization and management planning relates to the design of the organization and to the way it is to be managed
	5. Implementation and control have also to be planned; tasks assigned, performance monitored, adaptations made

it can be seen as a whole, but as 'a whole that can be divided into parts.' It is possible to take the organization apart; but then it could not perform its task. Human beings use the hand for writing; the hand is the operative part, but, as Ackoff says, 'A human body . . . can write, but none of its parts can.' In many cases, furthermore, what confronts decision-makers is not problems but something better called 'messes', that is, 'a *system of problems*'. These rather complicated statements lead Ackoff to the important conclusion that it is the attempt to deal with 'messes' which is the essential element in planning. Hence his picture of interactive planning can be expressed as in Figure 5, by a set of principles and steps or categories.[12]

This is a thoroughly systematic treatment of planning, and many other treatments of the subject follow basically similar lines. It is not difficult to see the pitfalls of unsystematic behaviour. It is obvious that levels of management are interrelated, that decisions in one part of an enterprise both impinge on other decisions and require connecting decisions to be made. This, after all, is reflected in Simon's statement, noted previously, that in an organization an executive makes his decisions with one eye on the matter in hand, the other on its organizational consequences. Ackoff's schema also has the merit of showing that planning requires a *portfolio* of plans dealing with each sub-section of the total process. In an earlier, more skeletal form, Ansoff had outlined what he called the 'generic structure of plans': see Figure 6 overleaf.[13]

Ackoff's analysis, Ansoff's generic structure, and the typical treatment of planning in the management literature contain important truths for managers. Clarity of intentions is likely to be helpful; how is it possible for managers to make effective decisions about, say, the departmental structure of their companies if they have not first clarified in their own minds what the companies are trying to achieve? Is it not obvious that if a company is thinking in terms of diversification, it should plan its programme of acquisitions and new ventures? In turn, as, for example, with British Petroleum, the general strategic plan for diversification will involve major planning for appropriate organizational change. Or consider what may seem a more distant example, what Curzon calls 'the management of the teaching situation'. He speaks of 'the essence of planning – the process of

FIGURE SIX
STRUCTURE OF PLANS

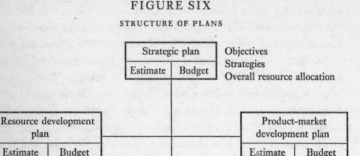

"thinking before doing, the devising of a line of action to be followed, the stages to go through and methods to be used." [14] Seen in this light, planning means to devise lines of action, and the resultant plans are expressed in decisions about priorities to be observed, resources to be deployed, rules to be followed, and procedures of monitoring and review to be determined.

Strategic planning has been conceived essentially as taking a long-term look, over a number of years, at the direction the corporation is taking. Corporate strategy is susceptible to change both in the light of problems which loom ahead in the external environment and new opportunities which are opening up. These are the changes which top management needs to identify or anticipate and against which it has to analyse the strengths and weaknesses of corporate resources. [15]

This approach entered into management thinking and practice and into the management textbooks – known there as ETOP (environmental threats and opportunities), analysis of internal strengths and weaknesses of the company – to the extent of becoming a stereotype of the kind of case presentation expected of students in business policy courses. It is a basically logical and rational way of looking at the strategic development of a corporation, and anybody who has taught courses of this kind will be familiar with the advantages of systematic analysis. A good many large organizations try to express this analysis in the form of quite detailed statements set out in, say, one-year, five-year or ten-year rolling plans.

But is the picture of corporate planning genuinely based on a realistic assessment of what actually faces managers when they come to consider the future of their companies? For example, is Ackoff's picture of organizations as systems an entirely realistic approach? If organizations are correctly described by Ackoff, then the efforts of managers should be directed precisely towards the kind of interactive, interdependent, rational planning which he recommends. The management emphasis will be, accordingly, on rational design: in fact, Ackoff puts it very expressively in the injunction to aim at interactive planning and prepare an *idealized redesign*, by which he means 'a design of the system with which the designers would replace the existing system *now* if they were free to do so.'[16] In other words, think out the best design, provided that it is technologically and operationally practicable. Then prepare an interactive plan which gets as close as possible to that design; do not concentrate on specific problem solving, but rather on dealing with 'messes', i.e. systems of problems.

Consider instead, however, another version of the organization, in which it is envisaged as composed of separate entities with separate, individual goals. Or consider the organizational complexity of the modern corporation which Tricker and others have outlined. This complexity of individuals, departments, sub-units, and large numbers of subsidiaries does not inherently invalidate the concept of corporate planning. It does suggest, however, that the top management of large corporations can contribute primarily through the setting of a limited number of guidelines, as Adrian Cadbury thought, and by choosing the general direction to be followed. But a further interesting consequence of complexity is that at the very top, boards of directors appear to spend less of their time on external issues of thinking ahead about strategy, and more time on internal issues of running the company, than either they or others might have thought desirable. Tricker shows this in two useful charts of the balance of board activities, Figures 7 and 8.

FIGURE SEVEN
BOARD ACTIVITIES — DESIRABLE

	Focus on the business	Focus on the shareholders/ stakeholders	
External issues	48	18	66
Internal issues	25	9	34
	73	27	100

FIGURE EIGHT
BOARD ACTIVITIES — ACTUAL

	Focus on the business	Focus on the shareholders/ stakeholders	
External issues	24	14	38
Internal issues	58	4	62
	82	18	100

In Tricker's sample of directors, the first chart (Figure 7) represents what they felt they should be doing, the second (Figure 8) what they thought they were really doing — *as per cent of their activity*. The tentative suggestion, or hint, is that they tended to concentrate on the internal aspects, e.g. the state of the order book, rather than on the strategic environment (and on the business they were running rather than on the shareholders).[17]

There are clearly several reasons for this, some bad, others good; and of course there is nothing sacrosanct about the percentages in those charts. One of the good reasons is a legitimate response to urgent continuing pressures; another is the genuine difficulty of comprehending a large and complex corporation in all its detail. Even if they were more virtuous in their attention to strategic issues, their major contribution would have to be in terms of guidelines. And two conclusions follow from this for management throughout the enterprise. Firstly, those guidelines are immensely important, as the discussion of strategy in the preceding chapter showed. What should be the general direction of the business and its overall use of financial resources; should it extend its interests overseas in, say, Australia or North America; what is the appropriate corporate structure? Secondly, the formulation of strategy and hence the requirements of a corporate plan will be the outcome of an interplay between various levels of the organization. Major planning commitments will have resulted from the planning decisions made by managers in divisions and subsidiaries, decisions on major projects and operations which will modify or partly predetermine the possibilities open or closed to the corporation as a whole. Thirdly, and perhaps most important, a corporate plan is better seen as a derivative of strategic ideas and not the other way round; a plan, in other words, is no substitute for creativity in entrepreneurship. It is true that ideas may emerge in the process of planning, because the mere exercise of analysing the environment and examining the strategic capacity of a company is a learning process. But it is more likely that creative ideas will emerge from other sources, from a less inhibited interplay of individuals and groups. The corporate plan, with all its limitations, may be a means by which managers can learn the implications of ideas in terms of the resources required to implement them.

This section of the chapter began with a reference to 'tidiness'. At the end of it, the management process is shown to be less holistic than the corporate plan appears on paper. This does not mean that there are no systematic relationships in an organization, nor that systematic analysis has no purpose. Management life would be hardly possible without it. But the reality of corporate structures is characteristically so complex that the management process is more disparate or diversified than might appear from the clear outlines of a plan.

Objectives and plans: plans and objectives

So far the emphasis has been on recognition of the importance of systematic analysis and on the systematic interdependence of the various parts of an organization. The corporate planning process has been viewed as perhaps more significant than the plans themselves, and attention has been drawn to planning as a process through which managers can learn about the environment, their opportunities and their problems. At the same time, the argument of the previous section encouraged some scepticism about overall planning for a corporation, particularly because of the stress laid on complexity in the modern business. This section is concerned with objectives and plans and with some further requirements for effective corporate planning.

Most texts on planning emphasize the significance of clarity and, preferably, simplicity of objectives. A distinction should be drawn, however, between specific goals and general statements; this point is interestingly brought out in K. K. Tse's study of Marks and Spencer, a company which many people, including management writers in Britain and the United States, often think of as a prime example of clear philosophy and objectives. Tse observes that

> Despite the idealistic overtones of some of the company's objectives, Marks & Spencer is a very practical and down-to-earth organization. It has persistently pursued certain key strategies over the past decades, but it did not start with any master blueprint or a comprehensive corporate plan. There was, and still is, a strong sense of direction in the minds of the management of the company, but it does not feel the need to draw up a statement of business mission as such. What it has laid down, however, is a set of fundamental principles which are to be the bases of all business activities.[18]

These principles, which Tse then outlines, were about quality and value for money, ways of working with the company suppliers, shopping comfort, operating efficiency, and human relations. Tse then adds that the secret of success is primarily that the company secured 'the total embracement of these principles by all levels of staff and their single-mindedness in focusing everyone's effort on those activities guided by these principles.'

Marks and Spencer is taken here only as a single example, and one which is perhaps rather specific to merchandise retailing. But it does suggest some wider connotations, as some further observations by Tse make plain. The founder of the company, Michael Marks, did not have a plan; he had a succession of ideas, some of which were responses to circumstances, such as his own penniless condition when he arrived in England. Or, again, his adoption of a fixed price policy – 'Don't Ask the Price, It's a Penny' – was the forerunner of the company's subsequent aims of high volume turnover with relatively low margins, finding quality products at reasonable prices. This followed from the fact that Michael Marks had always to search for a variety of products which could be sold for one penny, i.e. with a small profit margin and thus requiring high turnover. Much later in the history of the company, its chairman Simon Marks, only son of the founder, adopted in the 1920s the idea of a five-shilling price limit, because on a visit to America he had observed 'the wide variety of goods which the American chain stores were able to sell over their counters at the maximum price of a dollar.' The fundamental consequence of the price structure Marks and Spencer had thus chosen was that the company could not depend on what wholesalers would offer it. Instead, it had to search, actively, for products which would fit within the pricing structure it had adopted; hence the distinctive arrangements by which the company now obtains its products by direct relationship and careful consultation with manufacturers who make to specification.

This example has been given at some length because it illustrates some matters of wider interest than Marks and Spencer alone. Here, according to Tse, is not 'a comprehensive corporate plan', but nevertheless 'a strong sense of direction' and 'a set of fundamental principles'. In other words, the top management of the company formed a picture of where it was going without having to express this in the shape of a 'master blueprint'. But this picture was clearly of fundamental importance, and it established the system of values, the way of thinking, and the criteria for evaluating performance at all levels of the company.

There is another important general point indicated by this example. The practical objectives and detailed planning arrangements of the company were certainly fitted into the broad principles it had set for itself, but managers and others will recognize how one set of decisions was contingent on another. Michael Marks' market stall and uniform price of one penny enshrined the novel ideas of self-selection, self-service and simplified pricing. This governed his requirement for a wide range of low-cost supplies, a requirement which remained valid for his successor and promoted a whole range of objectives in supplier relationships. Objectives may certainly be set in advance and plans designed to attain them; but, as was seen in Chapter 4, objectives also emerge during the course of ongoing activity and plans have to be adapted to meet fresh sets of objectives.

Thus, looking at Marks and Spencer seems to provide an excellent instance of the importance of determining corporate purpose; Drucker regards this company as a prime instance of explicit strategic mission from which the operational objectives are derived. It is also clear from Tse's observations that the success of the company has been related to its success in transmitting its principles to all its staff. The implication is that managers are able to share the values and norms which are expressed in those principles. At the same time (and of course this is not a chapter about Marks and Spencer), it is clear that principles and ideas need not, and perhaps characteristically do not, emerge from a corporate plan. The planning process may generate new ideas because, by thinking about the company's environment and prospects, its strengths and weaknesses in resources, managers may develop fresh views and possibilities. The process may be one form of 'evoking mechanism'. But, logically speaking, it is the strategic concept which precedes the planning process; planning is no substitute for creativity.

Planning and the critics

In 1976 Lorange and Vancil, respectively at the Sloan School of Management MIT and the Harvard Business School, wrote that

Every business carries on strategic planning, although the formality of that process varies greatly from one company to the next. Conceptually, the process is simple: managers at every level of a hierarchy must ultimately agree on a detailed, integrated plan of action for the coming year; they arrive at agreement through a series of steps starting with the delineation of corporate objectives and concluding with the preparation of a one- or two-year profit plan. However, the *design* of that process – deciding who does what, when – can be complex, and it is vital to the success of the planning effort.[19]

Contrast this with the views expressed in the report of a conference held in France in 1983, which brought together more than four hundred corporate planners from business firms, consultancies and universities and elicited many striking points. The number of corporate planners had grown very appreciably; in big companies there were fifty per cent more than there had been two years earlier. They were well paid, the average salary of senior planners in the United States being $94,000. Yet the planners were sceptical – healthily so, says the report – about their existence and unsure about what they were doing. Management scholars, such as Henry Mintzberg of McGill University in Canada and Michael Porter from the Harvard Business School, saw much of the planning in companies as useless, too much 'useless planning by numbers' which stood in the light of creative generation of ideas. In practice, Mintzberg argued, the best managers, in the sense of those who are most effective in terms of developing new ideas and strategies, do not devote hours on end to formal organizing and planning. Nor is formal planning typically at the root of strategic success.

The source of ideas was frequently an individual in the company, or the outcome of internal crisis or of consensus – the last point being reminiscent of Lindblom and Quinn. As examples are cited Canada's national film board, which successfully backed the making of films for television after one film-maker had done so on his own, and Honda, the Japanese car manufacturer, which prospered, said Mintzberg, because it learned from its mistakes. It showed flexibility, and 'formal planning, often said to be the root of its success, has had little to do with it.' Both Mintzberg and Porter appear to have emphasized the importance of looking at what customers are saying and competitors are doing. Porter said that 'Planning has been viewed as an independent process, with too many flow charts', and that some

American companies were transferring the planning function from specialized staff to line management. This is in accord with what is, after all, a well-established view, that planning is too important to be left to planners; but perhaps it carries particular weight that it should be emphasized at a conference of corporate planners. The whole question of the understanding of planning and commitment to the plans seems to be associated, also, with wider questions of 'shared objectives', as, it appears, Volvo, IBM, Scandinavian Airlines, and many Japanese companies believe.

More immediately to the point here, however, was the apparent failure of strategic planning to produce results, a matter over which there is a good deal of uncertainty. Some of the failures appear to be due to the quality of the planning, and some to the competing demands of other activities and of crises; some appear to be due to chief executives who, according to research among French companies by Thomas Durand of the École Centrale des Arts et Manufactures, are blamed by planners for being 'too ready to alter corporate plans – or ignore them altogether – in the search for a fast buck.'

What are the key points in the report?

1. Formal planning is frequently, perhaps generally, not at the root of strategic success.

2. The best managers, in the sense of those who are most effective in terms of developing new ideas and strategies, do not devote hours on end to formal organizing and planning.

3. Strategic planning rarely produces results.

The reasons given in the report for the difficulties and failures which are experienced are, basically, that it is acutely difficult to forecast the course of events in the future, that it always takes longer than expected to implement plans, and that the quality of planning and implementation is inadequate. It will be remembered that the top executives of Tarmac were averse to 'number crunching', that is to say, corporate plans filled with numerical estimates, because the targets were never hit 'by a mile', so that they lost credibility. Managers simply did not believe the figures. Firms are subject to external shocks which it may be extremely difficult to see and act on in advance: the oil crisis of the 1970s is a case in point.[20]

These difficulties at the level of the corporate business enterprise are magnified at the wider level of the community. Hall shows this in his discussion of planning disasters. The Sydney Opera House, for example, he describes as perhaps 'a great architectural triumph' but 'without doubt a planning disaster', setting 'some kind of world record ... for time delay in completion and for cost escalation. Originally estimated in 1957 to cost just over $A7,000,000 and to be completed by January 1963, it was in fact finished in October 1973 at a cost of $A102,000,000'.[21]

Hall's book deals essentially with public goods, so that the 'actors' in his planning stories are community, bureaucracy and politicians, and this introduces a complexity of persons, motivation and considerations which go beyond the experience of most, if not all, business corporations. His account of the planning problems is not, however, without lessons for business, especially in big and complex corporations engaged in large, indivisible capital projects. They too are faced with the uncertainty which stems from the unknowability of the future, with the virtual unpredictability of exogenous shocks in the external environment, and with multiplicity of variables. Moreover, although business enterprises may not include the same set of actors as in the wider community, they do include a range of participants with a variety of individual, departmental and divisional perspectives and interests.

These arguments may seem curiously paradoxical and perplexing. Planning is used by managers in order to *reduce* the problems of uncertainty; after all, if managers could be absolutely sure about the future, why would they need to plan? Planning is *anticipatory* decision-making, and like all decision-making, it is needed precisely because choices have to be made without perfect foreknowledge of the likely outcomes. To choose a strategy and to formulate plans are means of providing some elements of stability and of matching the resources of an enterprise with its opportunities. Yet it appears also that uncertainty undermines the effectiveness and usefulness of the plans. Some American writers have argued, moreover, that the wide acceptance of strategic planning in the United States in the 1960s was a *consequence* of the comparative stability of that period, that stability is unlikely to return, and that there is unlikely to be any great improvement in the accuracy of long-term forecasts. Yet the textbooks of management continue to emphasize the significance of planning in the modern business corporation: Norton, in his exposition of the change process in BP, is explicit about the long-term perspective of the company and of the deliberate nature of its strategic decisions and planning. Can these apparent inconsistencies be ironed out?

Strategy and the uses of the planning process

The first point, a critical one to emphasize, is the distinction between strategic thinking and long-term corporate planning. Definitions are odious, but they are also helpful, and in this instance it is convenient to draw a distinction between the statement of company direction and the formal or informal plan which embodies the managerial steps required to achieve direction. The distinction between the two is not easily made in practice, because strategy and planning are interrelated and continuing processes, but conceptually it is a difference between the determining of direction and the designing of how to get there. Thus corporate strategy envisages the enterprise as it might be, and involves analysis of the threats and opportunities it may face. This is not only a textbook phrase; Cadbury Schweppes, for example, set up an 'Early Warning Group' composed of company members and outside academic members

> to monitor social, political and economic changes in the United Kingdom, so as to give an 'early warning' of possible *threats and opportunities for the Company* . . . The Group meets two or three times a year to consider recent trends, review specific topics and make general projections.[22] [Italics added]

A paper dealing with a number of environmental themes was explicitly termed a 'strategy paper'. This kind of thinking is at least one stage away from the formulation of a plan for a corporation, although it is clearly an input for the planning process, always assuming that the company is interested in the construction of a formal plan.

The second and equally critical point is that formal planning is what Quinn has termed a 'building block' in the strategic process. His list of the main contributions of systems of formal planning may be summarized as those of

- creating information networks
- extending managers' time horizons
- generating rigorous thinking about goals and resources
- systematic teaching about the future
- reducing the feeling of uncertainty and hence encouraging longer-term commitments
- stimulating 'longer-term "special studies"' which could be important in due time.

This last reference is noteworthy in the light of Quinn's finding that the special study of particular aspects of strategy was a primary agent of corporate strategic change. Thus management did occasionally engage in broadly-based 'total posture planning', i.e. looking at the global picture of the company as a whole. But the characteristic mechanism and the most directly important input from formal planning derived from the special study approach. For example, the major glass company Pilkington, once they had established their new float glass process, dealt with strategy for flat glass by setting up a Directors' Flat Glass Committee to look in broad terms at alternatives and their long-term consequences. In the experience of companies which Quinn observed, there could be said to be a strategic 'whole', but this was something which emerged or evolved through the incremental 'blending' of the strategies generated through the special studies.[23]

In emphasizing incrementalism, Quinn has not discarded the idea of formal planning systems; on the contrary, the third point here may be drawn from his comments that 'In most cases, even formal planning was actually part of an incremental process' and 'Formal planning practices themselves usually institutionalized a form of incrementalism.' These rather complex statements encapsulate several points which are of considerable importance in management. One is that within the broad assumptions or goals of the business, planning may typically develop 'from bottom up', thus using the expertise and securing the commitment of specialized levels throughout the organization. Another point is that plans may be thought of as 'living', making coherence out of decisions which managers had inescapably to make in the face of ongoing tasks and problems. And then formal planning provides a link between strategy and tactics, that is, the operational steps which are required to give effect to managements' intentions.

Seen in this light, corporate planning, formal and informal alike, can be an integral part of a process which is distributed through time and is a part of the management function throughout the organization. It is not, in other words, purely a matter for corporate planners. If, moreover, it is seen in this light, the strategies or sub-strategies which are developed in the component parts of enterprises can be seen as a portfolio of plans which may be co-ordinated at the centre but are not necessarily initiated there. Beyond these plans lie the detailed operating plans, the budgets and programmes which are required to move the company along chosen paths.

CHAPTER TEN

WHAT ABOUT NON-MARKET ORGANIZATIONS?

The analysis so far has not been confined to management in business enterprises; it has also referred to organizations in general. The main emphasis has been, nevertheless, on business, with the explicit or implicit assumption that management is working in market conditions. Strategy, for example, is seen to be concerned with product-market decisions in the framework of markets; strategic 'mission' is interpreted by Drucker and others as the identifying of a customer. But there is also a wide range of non-market and non-profit organizations where management has its own special characteristics which make particular demands on managers.

These organizations include a wide spectrum of activities which cover a substantial part of the modern economy; fire services and police forces are examples. Nationalized industries in Britain constitute a particular case because they were intended to be answerable to two masters, market and government, a dichotomy which has posed distinctive problems for the managers. A further set consists of what are very often, though by no means universally, managed as non-profit organizations, such as schools, universities and hospitals; they might also include certain types of organization of a charitable or advisory type staffed by voluntary personnel or by a combination of professionals and volunteers. The management of government departments and activities and of cities is another of the examples which lie within the ambit of this chapter, though they cannot all be considered in it.

There is now a very extensive literature on the special problems of management which are faced in non-market and non-profit organizations. It is interesting to observe the extent to which management education and training have spread beyond the business world to government service, hospitals administration, social welfare staffs, educational institutions, prison officers, and so on. Writing in 1975, Cyert said that

Despite the importance of hospitals and universities, there has been little attention given to these areas by business management scholars. The latter have tended to emphasize the business firm without looking for the possible transfer of knowledge. There is at least some evidence that this behavior is changing ... For the most part the management of universities has been ignored, and the administration of hospitals has been studied by specialists who usually do not have knowledge of the general management literature. The field of public administration has been a shining exception.[1]

The key reference in that paragraph is the phrase 'possible transfer of knowledge', that is to say, knowledge about management, for there was no lack of writing about the organizational characteristics of different types of institution, or at least of some of them. In his introduction to a *Handbook of Organizations* published in 1965, the editor James G. March observes that

There is scarcely a major philosopher, historian or biographer who has overlooked the management and perversities of organizations. The church, the army and the state had to be managed. Aristotle, Ibn Khaldoun, Thucydides, Caesar, Marsilio, Aquinas, and Bentham were not reluctant to solve such problems ...[2]

A whole section of the *Handbook* is devoted to a variety of organizations which include unions, political parties, public bureaucracies, military organizations, hospitals, schools and prisons. In his book *Cases in College Administration*, published in the United States in 1955, Ronald C. Bauer remarks that while education should not be confused with business or government, it makes demands on administration and administrative skills which are basically similar to those in any other kind of organization. The traditional categories of planning, co-ordination and control, for example, are just as much required to enable education as 'an institutional undertaking' to achieve its purposes. The cases in his book illustrate how deans and other college officers encounter decision situations analogous to those in business and government.[3]

Nowadays, certainly, it is quite usual for books of case studies for use in business policy courses to include cases on non-profit organizations, and courses and institutions now exist specifically devoted to the subject of management in non-business sectors.

Differences in fact or differences in principle?

A great deal of discussion about non-market and non-profit organizations is conducted as if there were a complete difference in kind between them and business-oriented institutions. They might even be regarded, it has been suggested, as 'domesticated organizations' whose basic organizational needs are catered for by the owners or patrons and rewarded or reined in as the mood of the owners and assessment of performance dictate. This may be so, but it is not as self-evident as is sometimes supposed; sometimes, what is thought of as a matter of principle is no more than a matter of fact, where fact means 'how things happen to be done at a particular time in a particular place'. For example, education and health services in Britain, as in many other countries, are mainly provided through the mechanisms of state and local authority and are funded through taxation. But they could, in principle, be provided in other ways and in practice are, to some extent, supplied to consumers who make direct payment for services rendered. Debate on this theme is, of course, at the heart of policy questions about 'privatization', which it is not the purpose of this chapter to consider. The reason for mentioning the topic here is to emphasize that there are alternative ways in which the supply of goods and services may be funded, but that in all cases there is a task of managing resources both effectively and efficiently, i.e. doing the right things in the right way, to employ Drucker's expressive distinction between the terms.

Not everybody would agree with this statement entirely; some people would argue that health care and university education, for example, raise ethical, philosophical and cultural questions of values which hardly apply in, say, the provision of 'ordinary' goods. From the point of view of management, however, what this means is that the statement of goals and the measurement of performance in certain types of organization present particular problems and may affect the particular ways in which the managers set about their jobs. Patterns of motivation may also differ significantly as between managers in market and non-market (non-profit) organizations, and institutional arrangements and conditions of job tenure may also have different features. There are attitudinal adjustments to be made, for example, when managers transfer from, say, the conditions of a postal system which is run as a government department to one which is an autonomous public corporation. This transition occurred in Britain in 1969, and some managers doubtless experienced a feeling of change from a 'service' organization to one which emphasized the 'business' more strongly. This did not mean, of course, that they discounted their service orientation, but that they now had a framework of business targets.

Despite the differences, there is a convergence of outlook and a similarity of problems. On the one hand, non-market organizations require knowledge of management, as the demand from a variety of institutions suggests – hospitals, social service bodies, local government, and others. On the other hand, *within* business enterprises there are motivational and management problems which are remarkably similar to those in the non-business world. For example, research and development departments in firms exemplify both categories of problem. The work goals of scientists may diverge from the marketing requirements of the business; scientists may be more interested in their standing in their peer group. The managing director of a large pharmaceuticals enterprise commented on the fact that research staff regarded management as a lower grade of work. Consequently, there was sometimes difficulty in transferring staff whose research productivity had fallen off to management functions (for which, moreover, they were not always well-suited). Just as it is difficult to measure performance in non-market organizations, so it may also be difficult in those departments in business corporations which do not come into direct contact with the market. Research and personnel departments are characteristic examples; the training function within personnel is another.

In looking at profit and non-profit organizations in the context of management, therefore, it is evident that neither a straightforward statement that they are fundamentally alike nor one which says that they are wholly unalike is quite true. There is a balance to be struck which may even differ from organization to organization, though to some extent the same problems of criteria and measurement are exposed to view in all of them.

Conflict of criteria [4]

One of the critical features which has been identified in the study of management is the problem of objectives or the criteria by which managers are to assess their performance. The management of any organization is clearly related to the purposes for which it exists; if these are ambiguous or conflicting, and if, relatedly, this applies to the measures of results, there are bound to be strains in the management and decision processes. Even in business enterprises, which are ultimately subject to the test of the market, there are inevitably such strains, partly because of conflict among multiple objectives, partly because not all objectives are quantifiable or unequivocal. For example, companies have been known to undertake fundamental research as a means of attracting good scientists to work for them, although there may have been reservations about the extent of their need for such research. In one company it was a joke (with an underlying seriousness) that they always had one scientist who could be pointed out to visitors as a sign that the company encouraged interest in basic work. How far attitudes and objectives of this kind can be quantified is doubtful, but it would be extremely misleading to ignore their importance. Or, again, different managers may either interpret objectives in different ways or make different judgements as to the relative importance of the various objectives in question.

Nevertheless, in organizations which depend on market response, there is the test of market survival, there are measurable outputs to set against inputs, and a mechanism for choosing between different outputs. This is what has been referred to as effectiveness – doing the right thing – as against efficiency, which means doing things right, again to emphasize the distinction. It looks beyond the question of reducing costs in any given activity, since it also asks the question: which activity should be undertaken? Thus, much of the discussion about the management of non-profit organizations turns on the question of how far it is possible to translate into their environment the types of measure which managers are able to use in the business world.

One commentator, discussing this in relation to such bodies as fire services and police forces, has pointed to the problem in all organizations of this kind that since the managers are not obliged to define their markets, or to meet demands related to markets, they may tend to think that their existence is, so to speak, self-justified. In the two cases cited, nobody would deny the need, but that is not the same thing as saying that the community at large will automatically continue to fund the services at any given level. Thus, for example, although a fire service can regard the needs for fire prevention and fire cover to be self-evident, it cannot be assumed that the volume of resources devoted to the service at a particular time will be regarded as sacrosanct. In fact, it appears that parts of national and local government in Britain are now actively investigating the costs and benefits of current standards of fire cover, examining present risk categories, and the implications of alternative manning arrangements.

The same commentator draws attention to the attempt by some police forces in Britain to adopt a form of Management by Objectives which they call Policing by Objectives, based on some statements of goals and of input and output measures. A similar attempt is now being made in the fire service in one area of the country.

These examples are interesting in themselves and also because, looking to the future, they show how the concepts of managing resources, of decisions as opportunity costs, and of accountability in the use of resources, are permeating a wide variety of organizations which have not always been seen in this light. This is not to come down in favour of or against any one approach, but it is to recognize a powerful trend towards emphasizing the management content of many areas of activity. Yet it raises problems for managers because it can be hard for them to see themselves wholly in business terms; the concept of service, for example, remains strong in some organizations in a sense which is almost independent of commercial factors and which can create genuine stresses. There are also significant examples of a related kind in the management experience of industries in the United Kingdom which were nationalized in the post-1945 period, notably coal, electricity, gas and transport. That experience exemplifies the problems encountered by management in seeking to meet the dual criteria of answerability to the market and accountability to the machinery of government.

The nationalized industries may thus be regarded as a kind of halfway house and a case study, from the point of view of management, between the opposite poles of market and non-market organizations. To the extent that their specific conditions still exist, they continue to raise topics which are relevant to managers, and some of the questions being discussed in a number of countries are pertinent even where there have been major changes in policy and organizational form. Furthermore, their experience shows how difficult it can be to try to separate the idea of policy in an organization from the management of its continuing operations.

The management picture can be put in the following frame of reference. A number of industries were nationalized to meet, in varying degrees, four main considerations or objectives which are particularly pertinent to management decisions:

1. All the industries were defined as basic, so that their performance and their investment, pricing and output decisions were significant for the whole economy.

2. They were generally less efficient than they could be and required larger-scale infusions of capital than it was thought would be provided by the private market.

3. It was held that they should provide uniform standards of service across the country, particularly in electricity supply and transport (both of these in respect of rural areas).

4. Industrial relations and personnel policies were to set a high standard: management was expected to match the best standards, even to set the pace for industry as a whole.

The chosen instrument for effecting policy was the public corporation, which people think of as a British invention and which certainly had some special qualities which were novel and striking. The corporation was to be, on the one hand, a part of the machinery of state control in the sense that it was ultimately responsible to Parliament through the minister; *but*, on the other hand, it was to be free to 'manage' the industry without intervention from the minister. *Thus, the idea of an autonomous public corporation rested on the assumption that a valid and practical distinction could be drawn between policy in a general sense and the day-to-day management of an enterprise.*

The relevance of this approach to the general question of management lies consequently in the question how far managers can be expected to answer to more than one master and more than one set of criteria. It has a bearing also on the relation between the top direction in any organization and the managers at other levels. In those sectors where the market ultimately rules, managers are directed and constrained by the need to identify the customer, even if Drucker's picture of the decision-making situation is over-simplified. In organizations which are strictly non-profit in orientation, whether these are public services or, for that matter, charities, attempts can be made to devise measures of performance and cost-benefit analyses. In the mixed world of public enterprise, neither situation applies precisely on its own, and much of the debate on nationalized industries, whether it is concerned with privatization or on how to improve their management irrespective of the form of ownership, turns on this question of dual criteria.

In the examples of the fire service and police force, it was evident that management might be tempted to envisage itself as responsible for a necessary service. If there are no unequivocal standards of assessment there is always the possibility that decisions about resources will be based on budgetary claims of 'last year plus x per cent'. If available resources are cut back, the experience is likely to be all the more disturbing. In the British public corporations, the problem presented itself for managers in this form: should their enterprises try to *interpret* the public interest or at least the wishes of the minister? It has certainly been argued of the earlier years of the National Coal Board that it allowed its domestic pricing policy to be influenced by the perceived requirements of government policy with respect to inflation. Or, again, is the distinction between policy and management really clear; for example, might not pricing policy in an industry be regarded in either light? Where does accountability lie if managers interpret the public interest without direct instruction from the minister: 'There has been no directive', he might say; 'it was a management decision of the board.' And yet his influence and that of the government in setting the parameters of management could hardly be denied.

The concern here is not, of course, with the pros and cons of nationalization or privatization but solely with the managerial questions which arise from the concept of dual criteria, of a double set of accountabilities. The public corporation in Britain was presented as a device which would combine business initiative and social accountability, commercial viability and community welfare. The management aspects which are illustrated still arise: for example, when there is debate on whether a postal business (in the public sector) should be a government department or an autonomous corporation, or on what regulatory mechanisms should be attached to management of large enterprises which have been privatized. Although much of the debate is conducted in terms of wide considerations of economic and social policy, it also has a management dimension. Indeed, the two overlap. Daunton, for example, in his recent study of the Post Office in Britain, gives the example that in 1980 the organization was criticized by the Monopolies and Mergers Commission for its failure to take management decisions because of prolonged consultations with unions; but, Daunton says, in the earlier post-war period they might have been criticized for the reverse. 'The managers of the Post Office', he observes, 'were following the policy of Governments of the day and accepting the general ethos of labour relations, both of which have changed radically in the 1980s.'[5]

The examples which have been considered so far illustrate also that managers always operate within certain constraints and that the introduction of a stronger awareness of management is tantamount to clearer recognition of what the constraints are. This should not be misinterpreted; a keen student remarked during a class in business policy: 'I don't think there should be so much emphasis on the need for a company to identify the *problems*; it is better to say, to identify the *opportunities*.' But constraints there nevertheless are, and management pressures draw attention to them. The nationalized industries in Britain illustrate one set of constraints, wholly public services another.

An interesting example was given in a discussion with senior personnel of a fire service who were attending a management course. They emphasized the importance of getting quickly to a fire: a minute could be absolutely crucial in the early stages, and increased resources which would enable the service to reduce the characteristic time taken to arrive on the scene would be extremely desirable. But since the supply of funds was not unlimited and there were competing demands on it, a management-conscious service – already, it is true, alert to efficiency – would have to look at its claims in terms of costs and benefits, explicitly as well as implicitly. Similar questions arose when a police force was considering how far it could use civilian resources in its organization so as to deploy its strictly police personnel most effectively. This is clarly a management problem in the disposition of resources.

What makes for difference and difficulty, therefore, is neither that there are no managerial decisions nor that these are always inherently different from those in business firms. It is that in the non-profit sector managers may be torn in more than one direction by the requirements of managerial efficiency, of professional or traditional concepts of service, and, in the case of certain kinds of public enterprise, by the explicit demands of dual criteria. For managers the area of non-profit organizations offers problems of singular interest and challenge – not more so than management in general, but of a particular character. Some of the challenges may be significantly affected by changes in general economic policy, but some of them will remain in one form or another in a number of the cases which have been illustrated here and in the management of a variety of health and educational services, of cities, and government departments.

A look at management in hospitals

In a chapter on case mix management contributed to a book entitled *Exploring New Vistas in Health Care*, R. Kenneth McGeorge, Chief Executive Officer of the Queen's University Faculty of Medicine in Canada, discusses this form of management in the Kingston General Hospital in Ontario. After describing problems which the hospital experienced in managing its affairs, McGeorge observes that

> In the search for better management tools, the hospital began a process of reorganizing and, in this context, recruited key people to key posts from the industrial sector . . . brought to the hospital a new sense of cost consciousness . . . This, together with a leading surgeon who had commenced graduate study in Business Administration and a Board Chairman from the auto industry, started an entirely new environment for cost analysis. People began to ask: What are we producing? (a question seldom posed in a hospital); and, Who causes the costs to rise or fall? The traditional answers, from the hospital sector, to these questions have been: We do not produce anything, but we treat patients. Furthermore, costs are controlled by cost center managers.[6]

This paragraph has been quoted partly because of its proposition that a hospital can be looked at as a producer of outputs by processes which can be managed in a business sense. It is also interesting from a management point of view, because it implies the question: what kind of organization is a hospital? As a stage in dealing with that extremely complex question, this section considers some comparatively recent writing, beginning with an interesting paper by Jeffrey Harris entitled 'The internal organization of hospitals: some economic implications', published in *The Bell Journal of Economics* in autumn 1977.[7] Harris was at the time a Clinical Fellow, Medical Services, Massachusetts General Hospital, as well as being Assistant Professor of Economics at Massachusetts Institute of Technology. His paper was written essentially as an economist but it was underpinned by his understanding of medical factors. The points considered here are those which bear on organization and management; in this regard, Harris's principal theses were:

- a hospital is really two separate firms in one, made up of medical staff, which he terms 'a demand division', and an administration, termed a 'supply division'.
- each of these firms 'has its own managers, objectives, pricing strategies and constraints.'

Harris then considers the stresses to which such a system is subject, especially when the demand from the medical staff outruns the short-run capacity provided by the administrators. By raising the problem in this way, Harris has focused attention on the critical management question in an organization which, as he says,

is a firm specifically designed to solve a complicated decision problem – the diagnosis and the treatment of illness. Because of the uncertainty inherent in human disease processes, this task requires an organization which can adapt rapidly to changing circumstances and new information.[8]

This is not unique to a hospital; what gives the situation a special character is that patient care is a matter for the doctor in his professional capacity. He requires that the individual patient shall receive penicillin, or a chest X-ray, or blood supply, and the ancillary services, e.g. the dispensary or pharmacy, are required to make provision. This provision it is the business of the hospital administration to make. Consequently, it can be seen that the demand for ancillary services and resources comes from the doctors, as and when they think them necessary; the supply has to be made available by the administration. There is thus a classic management problem of co-ordination in the difficult circumstances that doctors demand supplies 'on the spot' and the supplying departments have to respond at the time specified by the doctors.

The analysis made by Harris is paralleled in a paper by three other American writers, Cochran, Schnake and Earl, where they refer to the tendency of the medical staff 'to have primary allegiance to their profession rather than the organization.' They go on to say that a consequence of the way a hospital is structured, administratively and medically, is that .

within a hospital, there seems to be a tendency for dual management systems to develop. One's authority is based upon the position in the hierarchy and control over resources; the other's authority is based upon expertise and power derived from patients, other medical staff and the community.[9]

A further feature to which they draw attention also mirrors an aspect considered by Harris, in that hospitals tend to be structured around highly specialized departments and units, each competing for resources. The discrepancy between this condition and the concept of the organization as a whole, with overall values and goals, might be a potent source of disagreement. Moreover, the dual management may – in all probability will – have different objectives. The administration may be interested in keeping the hospital full, i.e. not wasting bed space; but 'Dr A cares little about an empty bed. But he will not be very happy if he cannot get one for Mr X', i.e. the individual patient who, in his opinion as a doctor, should have one. Given the doctors' insistence on particular requirements and, at the same time, the problem that capacity is not unlimited, Harris writes that

There are loosely enforced standards, rules of thumb, side bargains, cajoling, negotiations, special contingency plans, and in some cases literally shouting and screaming. As the hospital approaches full capacity utilization, these allocative devices become increasingly important.[10]

How far all these comments reflect a widespread reality in hospitals in the United States, Britain, or elsewhere is a matter for expert investigation and appraisal. Taken with other writing on hospital administration, they at least suggest some interesting pointers. To begin with, it is clear that many of these themes are neither unique to hospitals nor solely dictated by non-profit characteristics of hospitals. Problems of internal conflict and pursuit of sub-unit goals are familiar to managers in business organizations; so are competition for resources and difficulty in assessing performance and in allocating resources for some kinds of department within firms. There are, however, three aspects which, even if they are not entirely unique to hospitals, are very distinctive.

Firstly, there is the pervasive ethical element in medical care. There is what Harris terms a 'very sanctified atmosphere of "life and death" in which "doctor knows best".' It is not easy for a 'layman' to argue resources in these circumstances.

Secondly, the patient does not 'buy' a particular treatment; he buys 'being made well' by such treatment as the doctor prescribes for his particular case. Thus, while there are obviously general rules, each case may also be regarded as unique.

Thirdly, what the example of the hospital powerfully exemplifies is the problem of management in organizations which employ strongly professional groups. Hospitals are not the only places in which the management of professionals is to be found; schools and universities also have this experience, and so do business enterprises, e.g. in their R & D departments. But in hospitals, where 'doctor knows best', the possibility of two streams of thinking and the authority of the expert in relation to human medical welfare are both particularly significant. A hospital, perhaps more than any other organization, may be characterized as an organization which is a meeting-ground of various kinds of professional, seeking to effect their various purposes.

These considerations apply in hospitals whether they are private (in this sense operating within a market framework), voluntary or state-funded, as in the National Health Service in Britain. Nor is the question of professionalism unique to doctors; there are other professionals within hospitals, not least the administrators and paramedical staff, who have also become professionalized. A hospital is, indeed, a complex organization which involves the management in a variety of tasks and a variety of human interactions: administrators, doctors, nurses, pharmacists, catering and cleaning staffs, and the patients themselves, whose welfare is perhaps the one general goal to which all participants can be said to subscribe in general terms.

Does the non-profit element enter, then, into the picture? It does so in a significant sense for management in that, whereas in a market and profit-oriented organization there is an ultimate crucial requirement in the bottom line, to make sufficient profit (however that is defined), in a non-profit hospital that must ultimately be a subordinate consideration. Even for business enterprises, as has been pointed out, in the internal management of the organization, multiple objectives have to be considered. Drucker has referred to profit as a necessary condition of survival rather than as a goal of a business. But in a hospital, all the same, the heavy overlay of ethical considerations – the fact, as Perrow has expressed it, that hospitals 'attempt, as their primary task, to alter the state of *human* material', i.e. people, and that the arbiter of the patients' needs is the doctor – must have special consequences.[11]

Does this mean, in turn, that the transfer of management knowledge to which Cyert referred cannot be made in the case of hospitals? He certainly did not think so; he drew attention to the possibilities of forecasting patient demands, linking these to the quantity and types of resources required, and improving cost analysis. Considerable attention has been given to the development of performance standards for efficiency in management, and to wider thinking in strategic terms. The work of university and other centres for study and education in the management of health services is indicative of the modern trend, although to the extent that such work is carried out in specialized departments or centres, Cyert might hold that it reflects the conviction among managers that their business and problems are unique.

The task of management in the setting of the hospital is, then, a complex one. Some of the problems which arise can be the more effectively examined, and points requiring managerial action more readily detected, through improvement in management statistics and the employment of management techniques. It may be, also, that organization theory can make significant contributions to organization design which will have regard to the tendency of professionals to think of administration as a subordinate, service function. They are disposed to regard the organization as 'theirs', as consisting of them and their values, so that control should rest in their hands, with decisions made according to their standards of assessment.[12]

In one sense they are right, and many administrators are explicit in seeing it as their function to facilitate the work of the professionals. At the same time, however, since management involves choices in the use of finite resources, the relationship between the clinician, with his focus on individual patient welfare, and the manager or administrator looking at a budget, i.e. at financial constraints, is a crucial one. It seems probable that the link between clinical requirements and financial management has to be carefully established, and management information and thinking are not to be confined to only one group in the system.

Universities and management [13]

In *The Management of Nonprofit Organizations*, Cyert focused his main attention on universities, the management of which has a number of characteristics similar to those considered in the case of hospitals. Like a hospital, a university is populated by professionals. While the creation and transmission of knowledge in, say, economics or literature do not carry the same physical and emotional consequences as medical care of the sick, management has to reckon with the attitudes and ideals of academic professionalism in a tradition of academic freedom and administrative autonomy. Thus 'A University is precisely the kind of organisation in which the duality of professional and administrative goals is encountered.' Sir Robert Aitken, himself a vice-chancellor, writing on university administration, suggested three criteria by which the system might be evaluated:

The test of its aptness for its purposes is whether it allows the maximum freedom within wide limits, whether it finds the optimum point of balance between diffusion and concentration of responsibility, and whether it keeps the tension between individuals and the organisation down to a level that is healthy for both.[14]

Consider the points Aitken was making: a wide extent of judgement which members of the organization may exercise, a balance between responsibility at the centre and decentralization and dispersal of responsibility throughout the system, and a healthy level in respect of frictions and irritations as between the university as an organization and the member as an individual. Now consider the relation of those criteria to the conditions in which they were written, conditions of almost continuous expansion in universities and university resources. In those circumstances, there were of course major demands made on management and administration; for example, there were very large building programmes to be initiated and brought to completion, courses to be organized and developed, staff to be recruited, libraries to be set up and expanded. The management of expansion is neither easy nor wholly painless, as many businessmen would probably testify. Even within organizations which are stable, i.e. neither growing nor contracting overall, there may be management decisions to be made since changes may be taking place all the time within and as between departments.

Nevertheless, in the case of universities at least, the years of expansion can hardly have required too many painful decisions; the dean of a faculty who asks for, say, eight new lectureships and is allocated seven can hardly feel seriously distressed. Expansion within a budget-funded organization does not eliminate differences about resource allocation, but the tensions are eased by the emollient of 'something for everybody'. Even more important are two other points. The first is that in organizations like universities the period of expansion masked the absence of a managerial structure capable of taking painful decisions. The second, related point is that in universities, even more than in other kinds of organization, management and administration have rested on a balance of understanding among lay members, academics and administrators. There has been, in other words, a negotiated environment, a shared reality, implicit or explicit, among the participants. (The same argument has been applied to hospitals.) How deeply this shared reality runs is perhaps not truly tested until the relative security and comfort which have hitherto been enjoyed are 'ruptured both by external financial pressure and by a challenge to the academic professional assumptions . . .'[15]

The management of a university thus displays a number of characteristics which are found in business too, but it does so rather sharply. This is evidenced in the plurality of its goals and the central significance of a set of values: academic freedom, scholarship, and a sense that there is an equality which underlies membership in a community of scholars and teachers. At the same time, a university is a system of employment with various income-earning groups and a set of industrial relations. It is commonly, though not always, budget-based, drawing income largely from public funds and not from revenues from market performance. The 'idea' or 'ideal' of itself is in a way independent of its direct function or utility: but it also has to help prepare students to earn a living which depends on the requirements of employers.

Which are the critical characteristics from the point of view of management? Some writers emphasize the importance of the budget-based element in service institutions, that is, that their primary revenue comes from an allocated budget and not from sales in a product market. It has been said, indeed, that there are differences within universities between the attitudes of departments which are funded in this way, the general pattern in British universities, and those which depend essentially on fee-earning through the provision of courses for managers and other groups. These are differences concerned with finance, 'marketing' and relations with the 'customer'.[16] Other writers have emphasized the significance of professional autonomy: Lotte Bailyn, for example, refers to the freedom to choose the problems on which to work, to pursue them independently of directives from anywhere except the precepts of a discipline, and to publish freely the results of research. This set of values is inculcated and reinforced by the university, as educator and employer of scientists ... Such autonomy requires an organizational context geared to its expression, and technical specialists dedicated to the pursuit of science for its own sake.[17]

Another element which has been identified is the difficulty of measurement stemming apparently from the non-market feature of universities, which creates difficulty in decisions about resource allocation as between different faculties and departments. This may go together with 'A belief in self-regulation – fellow professionals are best qualified to judge the work of a professional . . .'[18]

It has already been observed that the problems of management in a university have their parallels in the business enterprise, and it could be argued that if all universities were to be privatized and placed in a market-oriented context, the differences between academic management and business would disappear. Even with less dramatic change, a non-profit organization could increase the rationality of its resource allocation process, according to Cyert, if it undertook the admittedly very difficult task of developing 'a comprehensive set of goals' from which it could, in turn, arrive at a set of priorities. Similarly, Cyert draws attention to the possibility of measuring performance: for example, the quality of research in a department can be assessed from the record of publications by its members in recognized journals of excellence. Teaching can be made subject to certain kinds of evaluation: the ability to attract good students is some demand index of the standing of a university or department.

Lotte Bailyn, in the quotation about academic scientists, was contrasting the orientation of a university with that of an industrial research laboratory, which is 'subject to controls emanating from the business goals of the parent organization', and argues, further, that 'most of the lab's employees do not desire such professional autonomy.'[19] How far that is true, business managers may be able to judge from their own experience. As far as universities are concerned, at least in the form in which they are generally financed in Britain and elsewhere, there is a particular management situation in that academic autonomy combined with academic involvement in the administrative processes both play a part. It is put by Cyert again when he draws attention to the contrasting claims of economic efficiency and professional attitudes in non-profit organizations. Experience bears out his warning that managers in those organizations in their concern for efficiency have also to be sensitive to this contrast. The value system of the professionals will suffer some shocks because the managerial pressure for efficiency may confront the organization with choices which seem to run counter to their view of its purposes and their standards. But insofar as certain values constitute what Cyert calls 'the essential nature of the organization' they have to be taken into account when managers are making their legitimate efforts to allocate resources efficiently.[20]

Managers in universities as one form of this type of organization are thus involved in a complex situation. Who, indeed, are the managers? Presumably the answer is: vice-chancellors, deans of faculties, heads of departments, finance officers, working within a formal structure of committees and procedures. But part of the management decision process is made by academics, operating as a collegial community. But yet, again, this community may not be homogeneous; decision-making may be political, in the sense in which the term has been used earlier in this book, of different interest groups engaged in a bargaining process. Furthermore, whereas Cyert has commented that non-profit organizations tend to be centralized because of the absence of a system of profit centres, they may in fact be decentralized because informed decision-making would require more knowledge in more areas than the senior administrators in fact possess. When financial constraints generate greater centralization, the relation between the sub-units and the centre may become tense; the balance which Aitken thought necessary may become difficult to sustain.

A note of summary

The organizations which have been considered in this chapter all exemplify, to a greater or lesser degree, particular problems for management which are generated by the absence of a business market test or, in one case, the combination of market and political tests, the prominence of general values and especially of professional codes, and the interplay between the exigencies of economic efficiency and professional autonomy. Each sector could be considered in much greater detail, and other instances could be discussed: the management of social service organizations, of government departments, and of cities are major areas. Each of them would display its own, special characteristics, all would also show some common ground. Cyert, it was observed, implicitly warned against the claim of uniqueness, 'our case is different'; the experience of non-profit organizations is also a warning that management should not be regarded as a universal code to be applied without regard to possible differences in underlying assumptions.

CHAPTER ELEVEN

THEMES FOR THE FUTURE

It became fashionable some years ago to refer to management as an 'intellectual challenge'. In Britain, this was part of a blossoming of management education which has been accompanied by continuing debate about the meaning of management and how it can be analysed and taught. There *is* an intellectual challenge in the direct sense that managerial decisions about resources and organization require a great deal of thought: they need the use of intellect. A further point is that the study of ideas opens up fresh avenues of thought and may suggest hitherto unexplored courses of action. Sometimes study makes explicit those ideas which have implicitly been guiding managerial action and which, when brought into the open, may call for reconsideration.

The source of the challenge may be the teacher or research worker, in universities, business schools, colleges and training institutions in industry and commerce. It may be the managers themselves, or the non-executive member of a board who asks 'Why do we do it this way?' and does not rest with the reply 'We always have done.' If a company reacts to a drop in sales by adjusting its prices or its advertising expenditure, it is making an assumption (which it hopes is correct) that sales are responsive to prices or advertising in a particular way. Experience may justify the course of action or it may not; the hypothesis is tested by experience. Or, again, the attempt to define the term 'strategy' is a crucial step in the task of formulating it better, and in deciding who should be involved in formulating and implementing it. Clarification of the concept of planning and of its function in a business is a stage in the allocation of planning responsibilities. To explain, if not to define, what is meant by an organization is to try to analyse the ways in which disparate individuals and departments can be brought together within a shared framework of understanding and activity.

When Alfred Sloan wrote of the organization of General Motors, as he saw it, that it was a system of 'federal decentralization', and referred to the problem of reconciling central control with divisional autonomy, he was describing a practical situation. At the same time, however, he was discussing a set of ideas about the effective way to organize a large and complex enterprise.[1] The characteristic fragmentation of management life and the time-consuming impact of current problems may frustrate attempts to engage in longer-term thinking, but they do not invalidate the need. Tricker's observations on the use of time by boards of directors, and their views on how they thought they *should* be using their time, are tentative but nevertheless instructive. The arrangements which companies make to enable managers to consider the business, unhindered by everyday constraints and pressures, or the research programme set up by Cadbury Schweppes with its Early Warning Group to 'monitor social, political and economic changes in the United Kingdom', reflect the importance attached to analysis as a prerequisite of business strategy.

Rosemary Stewart observes that her discussions with managers showed:

first, that there are remarkably few books on management, apart from the purely anecdotal, that most managers do not find either too ponderous, or too theoretical, to be readable; secondly, that managers are interested in descriptions of social research into management practice and problems. (Social research is the study of people, both as individuals and in groups.)[2]

There is room for all kinds of books and perhaps the key point is that managers have to *practise* management and that, consequently, they are especially interested in research and theory which they can clearly relate to the management environment. They might feel inclined to 'avoid the teachings of speculators whose judgements are not confirmed by experience.'[3] The intellectual challenge is not just an intellectual exercise.

Is it universal?

Writing in 1979, seventeen years later than her observation quoted above, Stewart drew attention to the increase in the number and types of people who now thought of themselves as managers – 'even bishops', she remarks.[4] A significant aspect is that not only is much more attention being paid to the idea that many non-business organizations are management systems, but that their members have come to see themselves as managers. The extension of management thinking and education for civil servants, nurses, hospital administrators, prison officers and other groups both reflect and accentuate this development.

In this sense, there is a universe of management in which are to be found a variety of organizations: in all of them, problems of resource allocation, organizational design and human relationships present themselves for analysis and solving. For as long as organizations have existed to bring people together for the accomplishment of purposes which have been defined as those of the organization and for the achievement of their own, joint purposes, there have been the tasks of managerial co-ordination and change. The biblical Moses, for example, might be described as a supremely gifted manager of men, defining his strategic objectives, adapting his techniques to the quality of the resources available to him, establishing formal rules of conduct, and creating a corporate identity for the group. In the wilderness, he learns from his father-in-law the importance of decentralization and delegation, and later he shows his understanding of the problem of succession in his choice of Joshua, soldier and administrator – not, like himself, prophet and lawgiver.

This example may seem to be offered with tongue in cheek; but in spite of the unusual context, it is a valuable demonstration of the general and widespread character of the management function and the managerial experience. The analogous reasoning applies in the discussion of different kinds of organization, business and non-business, profit and non-profit. It is put in its strongest form in the argument that management is management and that good managers are not constrained by the particular nature of an organization. Thus they are transferable between different organizations, especially above a certain level in the hierarchy of management.

It would be carrying the argument too far, however, to insist that there is something called 'management' which manifests itself in the same way in all circumstances and all organizational conditions. At different times and in different places, the boundaries of managerial action will also be different: cultural environment, technology, size and type of business, existence of management techniques, managerial styles, will affect not only the ways in which management problems are handled, but also how they are perceived. The variety of business firms is as striking as the general similarities in management problems. The discussion of non-profit organizations takes the point further, illustrating as it does the range of considerations to which managers have to be sensitive in a world of professional autonomies. Cyert emphasizes the importance and possibility of using management knowledge to improve efficiency in use of resources in the non-profit environment. Some people might call this being more business-like, to the extent, it might be argued, that a change in the institutional framework by introducing exposure to the market would, in fact, enforce it. Even in the area of the hospital, it has been suggested in some recent American writing that there are significant changes which have led to hospitals having to face competitive pressures which affect those in both the profit and non-profit sectors.

Nevertheless, the institutional context has to be taken into account; even if it were to change appreciably, the special features *within* non-profit organizations which create difficulty and ambiguity in measurement of performance, the significance of professional relationships and the dual management to which Harris suggested this gives rise, all require particular sensitivity on the part of managers. It may be, also, that the structure of organization which is appropriate to a business enterprise may be inappropriate to this kind of duality; the balance between hierarchical and lateral relationships may be a different one. Adrian Cadbury, in a lecture given in 1969, saw the problem as one of 'co-ordinating the specialists and seeing that their priorities are set from a total company point of view . . . The same situation arises outside business', he said 'in fields like hospital management and urban planning.'[5]

Cadbury was far-sighted in his reference to those areas of management, and right in specifying the problem as one which transcended the boundaries of business. It does not follow, however, that it arises with the same emphasis or that it can be dealt with in precisely the same way in a hospital or university as in a business corporation.

Choices and managerial planning

People who are trained in the study of economics come to think naturally in terms of making choices, and so do managers, whether their formal training has been in economics or not. Perhaps this is a somewhat optimistic view of both groups, but it can be expressed with some confidence, nevertheless, in these words of Joseph Bower:

the essential aspect of a technocratic management system is not profit. It is selectivity. Profit is simply a marvelously simple tool by which selectivity can be guided . . . If the environment changes, survival may require the organization to alter its purpose and transfer resources. *The organization's life can be distinct from its purpose at any particular time*. Thus, as consumer electronics becomes more competitive and as its work force grows older, Sony has moved into life insurance and cosmetics – one to ensure cash flow, the other to provide less physically demanding employment for its organization. Sony is an organization of people, not merely a producer of television sets and hi-fis. Similarly, universities that were built to train preachers or farmers now train engineers, lawyers, and business managers.[6] [Italics added]

Bower wrote that passage in the context of the contrasted field of management in politics, but his words are also relevant to the topics of innovation and corporate planning. The selectivity of which he writes is not something which takes place automatically within the firms; it requires decisions and courses of action by managers. When Bower says that 'Sony has moved into . . .' or Norton (see p. 108), says that BP adopted a strategy of diversification, it means that the responsible executives in Sony and BP behaved in such a way, took such decisions, that the results described took place. This has been emphasized in this book, obvious though it may perhaps appear, because it brings out the positive feature that management within firms requires decisions by its members and that, by implication, the awareness and quality of managers and decision procedures are important in organizational performance.

In his lecture, Cadbury refers to divisions which have to be reconciled, 'one of the most intransigent being between planners and operating managers.' Someone, he says, has to be looking ahead; how is the detachment from day-to-day matters which this requires to be matched with proper contact with realities?

How can the constraints, which must exist in practice for any organisation, be applied without stunting the planner's imagination and narrowing his conceptual framework? This is one aspect of a fundamental dilemma, which is represented by the need for a successful organisation to define its objective with precision, while having an equal need to be free-thinking and imaginative, if it is to survive in a rapidly changing environment.[7]

There is then the further problem in planning how to give practical effect within the organization to the long-term thinking. There is a gap to be bridged between long-term conclusions and the dictates of ongoing activities: moreover, the organizational structure may have to be adapted to the fresh requirements.

Those are general topics with which managers at various levels in many business and non-business organizations are obliged to grapple. At the same time, each individual organization has its own perception of the external environment and its own internal environment. Thus even if there were a unique general answer to all the problems (which of course there is not), it would still have to be interpreted into the individual organization; managers have to decide what they are going to do in their own organization. This is not to say that there are no general ideas on techniques; obviously there are, and they are tremendously useful. It is only to focus attention on the need to translate them into courses of action for the specific organization.

It is clear from Cadbury's remarks also, and from the problems of corporate planning, that at the heart of successful management lies the question of imagination and innovative spirit. Managerial planning is an instrument, not an alternative to strategic imagination. While the uncertain and unknowable characteristics of the future have been delineated, this is not in the least to say that this rules out decisions. On the contrary, it is what makes creative decisions so important and is why a voyage of ideas is so important for management.

GENERAL BIBLIOGRAPHY

The following is a short bibliography of books and journals on management and organization in general and on particular aspects which readers may wish to explore.

ROSEMARY STEWART, *The Reality of Management*, Pan Books in association with Heinemann, London, revised edition 1979.
The Reality of Organizations, Pan Books in association with Macmillan, London, 1972.
Both books are of modest length and are useful introductions to the topics, based on extensive discussions with managers.

PETER F. DRUCKER, *Management*, Pan Books in association with Heinemann, London, 1979. An abridged version of *Management: Tasks, Responsibilities, Practices*, this is, nevertheless, a lengthy book written in vigorous style and covering a wide range of subjects, with numerous examples.
Management Cases, Heinemann, London, 1978. Fifty short cases dealing with management situations and problems.

CHARLES B. HANDY, *Understanding Organizations*, Penguin Books, Harmondsworth, third edition, 1985. An extensive study of what organizations are and how they function, using many apt and interesting examples.

J. O'SHAUGHNESSY, *Business Organization*, George Allen and Unwin, London, 1966. A straightforward study of different approaches to management and supervision.

W. DAVID REES, *The Skills of Management*, Croom Helm, London, 1984. A practical approach to the manager's job and the specific skills required, e.g. in selection, appraisal and counselling, etc.

IVAN L. ROBERTSON and GARY L. COOPER, *Human Behaviour in Organisations*, Macdonald and Evans, Plymouth, 1983. A basic account intended for diploma and undergraduate students of management taking a course in occupational psychology.

A. KAKABADSE, *The Politics of Management*, Gower, Aldershot, 1983. Deals with the internal behaviour of organizations and the interactions among people at work; illustrated with many examples.

RICHARD TANNER PASCALE and ANTHONY G. ATHOS, *The Art of Japanese Management*, Penguin Books, Harmondsworth, 1982. For the reader who might like something about management in a different environment, which has excited a great deal of interest in recent years, this is a very readable account.

Journals

The following are a few of the numerous journals in the field of management and organization studies.

Journal of General Management: primarily for senior managers and administrators who wish to keep in touch with ideas and practice in management, and for students and executives attending courses in management.

Journal of Management Studies: includes a great deal of research material in the area of organization studies in business and non-business organizations: both general and on specific, applied topics.

Strategic Management Journal: designed for practising managers and academics: deals, in an advanced way, with a wide range of topics in the theory and practice of strategic management.

Long Range Planning: the journal of the Society for Strategic and Long Range Planning and the European Planning Federation. Applied articles with international coverage.

Harvard Business Review: extensive coverage of management topics of interest both to academics and to managers; ideas placed in a relevant and practical context.

California Management Review: research articles in subjects related to business: also business surveys.

NOTES

Chapter 1: Introduction

1. See the General Bibliography, pp. 203–4.

2. Eberhard Witte, 'Field Research on Complex Decision-Making Processes – The Phase Theorem', *International Studies of Management and Organization*, Vol. II, No. 2, Summer 1972.

Chapter 2: What is management all about?

1. Herbert A. Simon, *Administrative Behavior*, The Free Press, New York, second edition, 1965, p. xvii.

2. Thomas Tilling was later acquired by another company.

3. Winston Churchill, *The Second World War*, Cassell, London, 1951, Vol. IV, Chapter III, p. 43.

4. H. I. Ansoff, 'Towards a Strategic Theory of the Firm' in H. I. Ansoff (ed.), *Business Strategy*, Penguin Books, Harmondsworth, 1969, p. 12.

5. A. L. Minkes and D. G. Tucker, 'J. A. Crabtree: A Pioneer of Business Management', *Business History*, Vol. XXI, No. 2, July 1979, *passim*, but see especially p. 204.

6. L. B. Curzon, unpublished chapter on 'Communication', made available to the author with kind permission to quote from it.

7. Charles B. Handy, *Understanding Organizations*, Penguin Books, Harmondsworth, third edition, 1985, Part Two, Chapter 12, pp. 373–4.

8. Lord Franks, *British Business Schools*, British Institute of Management, London, 1963.

9. Peter F. Drucker, *Management*, Pan Books in association with Heinemann, London, 1979, *passim*.

10. Rosemary Stewart, *The Reality of Management*, Pan Books in association with Heinemann, London, revised edition, 1979, Chapter 4, p. 76.

11. Rosabeth Moss Kanter, *The Change Masters*, Unwin Paperbacks, London, 1985, Chapter 1, p. 27.

Chapter 3: Decisions and decision-making

1. David J. Teece, 'Economic Analysis and Strategic Management', *California Management Review*, Vol. XXVI, No. 3, Spring 1984, p. 91.

2. Terence Hutchison, 'Our Methodological Crisis' in Peter Wiles and Guy Routh (eds.), *Economics in Disarray*, Basil Blackwell, Oxford, 1984, Chapter 1, p. 4.

3. H. A. Simon, 'Administrative Decision Making', *Public Administration Review*, Vol. XXV, No. 1, March 1965 (also as Reprint No. 189 of the Carnegie Graduate School of Administration).

4. Simon, ibid., p. 31.

5. Simon, ibid., p. 35.

6. Minkes and Tucker, op cit., p. 202.

7. Henry Mintzberg, 'The Manager's Job: Folklore and Fact' in S. J. Carroll, F. T. Paine, J. B. Miner, *The Management Process*, Macmillan, New York, second edition, 1977, Part II, p. 52 (reprinted from *Harvard Business Review*, 53, No. 4, 1975).

8. H. A. Simon, *The Shape of Automation*, Harper and Row, New York, 1965, Part III A, p. 53.

9. Simon, ibid., p. 55.

10. Simon, *Administrative Behavior*, Chapter VIII, p. 155.

11. Brian J. Loasby, *Choice, Complexity and Ignorance*, Cambridge University Press, 1976, Chapter 5, *passim*, but see especially p. 80.

12. The author is indebted to Dr Simon Vickers for helpful discussion of this point.

13. Kenneth J. Arrow, *The Limits of Organization*, Norton, New York, 1974, Chapter 3, p. 47.

14. Simon, 'Administrative Decision Making' (op. cit.).

15. Witte, op. cit., p. 180.

For an interesting study of decision processes, see Bernard M. Bass, *Organizational Decision Making*, Irwin, Homewood, Illinois, 1983.

Chapter 4: Step-by-step in decision-making

1. Charles E. Lindblom, 'The Science of "Muddling Through"', *Public Administration Review*, Vol. XIX, Winter 1959.

See also: *The Policy-making Process*, Prentice-Hall, New Jersey, second edition, 1980. 'Strategies for Decision-Making', *University of Illinois Bulletin* (Department of Political Science: Edward J. James Lecture on Government), 1971. 'Still Muddling, Not Yet Through', from *Public Administration Review*, Vol. 39, No. 6, November/December 1979, pp. 517–26.

2. Lindblom, 'Strategies for Decision-Making', pp. 4–5.

3. T. Sorenson, *Decision-Making in the White House*, Columbia University Press, New York, 1963. (Lindblom is referring to pp. 18–19 of this book.)

4. Lindblom, 'Strategies for Decision-Making', p. 5.

5. James B. Quinn, *Strategies for Change: Logical Incrementalism*, Irwin, Homewood, Illinois, 1980, Preface, p. x.

6. M. L. Gimpl and S. R. Dakin, 'Management and Magic', *California Management Review*, Vol. XXVII, No. 1, Fall 1984, pp. 125 and 135.

7. Lindblom has made it clear that what he has in mind is that problems which become too big for the minds of the decision-makers have to be simplified and decision-making strategies devised so as to make the most of rationality – but it is bounded rationality.

8. Quinn, op. cit., Chapter 2, pp. 14–15.

9. Ansoff, 'Towards a Strategic Theory of the Firm' (op. cit.).

10. A particular pattern is not, of course, immutable. It has been reported that Cadbury Schweppes 'plans to sell most of its British food-and-beverages division – which does not include Schweppes soft drinks – to its managers. This follows a similar management buy out . . . of the company's health-and-hygiene business' (*The Economist*, 18–24 January 1986, p. 56).

11. Sir Anthony was speaking at the Industrial Seminar at Birmingham University.

12. Referred to in a lecture given in Hong Kong in 1984 by Dr Victor Fung, Managing Director of Li and Fung Ltd, the company concerned.

13. Lindblom, 'Strategies for Decision-Making', pp. 5–6.

14. A. L. Minkes and C. S. Nuttall, *Business Behaviour and Management Structure*, Croom Helm, London, 1985, *passim*.

15. M. A. Maidique, 'The New Management Thinkers', *California Management Review*, Vol. XXVI, No. 1, Fall 1983, p. 153.

Chapter 5: Are decision-makers really rational?

1. The Free Press, New York, second edition, 1965. *Administrative Behavior* may be regarded as a pioneer work in the field in its analytical emphasis and its treatment of rationality. Simon's work in this area and on decision-making embraces a wide range of other writings. See, e.g., *The Shape of Automation*,

Harper and Row, New York, 1965, and *Reason in Human Affairs*, Stanford University Press, 1983.

It is curious that when Simon was awarded the Nobel Prize in Economics a few years ago, a commentator described him as the first *non-economist* to receive it.

2. Simon, *Administrative Behavior*, Introduction, p. xxiii.

3. Simon, ibid.

4. Simon, ibid.

5. See Andrew C. Stedry, 'Market Versus Behavioral Theories of the Firm and Basic Managerial Research', *Management Sciences Report No. 70*, Graduate School of Industrial Administration, Carnegie Institute of Technology, April 1966, p. 11, for the reference to this example ascribed to Simon.

6. Simon, *Administrative Behavior*, p. 68. Minkes and Nuttall, *Business Behaviour and Management Structure* (op. cit.).

7. Teece, 'Economic Analysis and Strategic Management' (op. cit.), pp. 105–6. The reference to Nelson and Winter is to R. R. Nelson and S. G. Winter, *An Evolutionary Theory of Economic Change*, Harvard University Press, 1982.

8. P. F. Drucker, *Management Cases*, Heinemann, London, 1978, Part One, Case Number 1.

9. Sir Geoffrey Vickers, 'Positive and Negative Controls in Business', *Journal of Industrial Economics*, Vol. VI, No. 3, June 1958, p. 178.

10. Simon, op. cit. R. M. Cyert and J. G. March, *A Behavioral Theory of the Firm*, Prentice-Hall, Englewood Cliffs, New Jersey, 1963.

11. Drucker, *Management* (op. cit.), Chapter 4, pp. 55–6.

Chapter 6: The innovative manager

1. Michael L. Tushman and William L. Moore (eds.), *Readings in the Management of Innovation*, Pitman, Marshfield, Massachusetts, and London, Preface, p. xi.

2. Bela Gold, 'Values and Research', Research Program in Industrial Economics, Reprint No. 8, School of Management, Case Western Reserve University, p. 409. Chapter reprinted from Kurt Baier and Nicholas Rescher (eds.), *Values and the Future*, The Free Press, New York/Collier-Macmillan, London, 1969.

3. J. E. S. Parker, *The Economics of Innovation*, Longman, London, 1974, Chapter 5, p. 81.

4. Gordon R. Foxall, *Corporate Innovation*, Croom Helm, London, 1984, Chapter 1, p. 14.

5. Rosabeth Moss Kanter, *The Change Masters*, Unwin Paperbacks, London, 1985, Chapter 1, p. 21.

6. Drucker, *Management*, Chapter 7, p. 99.

7. W. E. G. Salter, *Productivity and Technical Change*, Cambridge University Press, second edition, 1966.

8. Stewart, *The Reality of Management*, revised edition, 1979, Chapter 10, p. 167.

9. Foxall, op. cit., Chapter 11, p. 247.

10. Tom Burns and G. M. Stalker, *The Management of Innovation*, Tavistock, London, Social Sciences Paperback, 1966.

11. A. L. Minkes and G. R. Foxall, 'The Bounds of Entrepreneurship: Interorganisational Relationships in the Process of Industrial Innovation', *Managerial and Decision Economics*, Vol. 3, No. 1, 1982, pp. 41-7: see especially pp. 44-6.

12. Topics of this kind are extensively discussed in Foxall, *Corporate Innovation*, *passim*.

13. Drucker emphasizes the question of identifying the customer's unsatisfied wants, and gives as illustration Sony's introduction of portable transistor radios. It was Bell Laboratories, not Sony, who developed the transistor; but it was Sony, unlike the other manufacturers, who saw the possibility of a new growth market by asking what were the wants which were not satisfied by the existing equipment. What were the unsatisfied wants which they could meet? See Drucker, *Management*, Chapter 5, p. 83.

14. Christopher Freeman, *The Economics of Industrial Innovation*, Penguin Books, Harmondsworth, 1974, Chapter 5, p. 169.

15. Alfred D. Chandler, Jr, *Strategy and Structure*, MIT Press, Cambridge, Massachusetts, 1962, Introduction, p. 15.

16. Chapter 10 discusses this topic in further detail in the context of non-market organizations.

17. Stephen Cotgrove and Steven Box, *Science, Industry and Society*, Allen and Unwin, London, 1970, Chapter 6, *passim*, but see especially pp. 131-6.

18. James Brian Quinn and James A. Mueller, 'Transferring Research Results to Operations' in *Readings in the Management of Innovation*, Pitman, Marshfield, Massachusetts, and London, 1982, p. 64 (reprinted from *Harvard Business Review*, January–February 1963).

19. Kanter, op. cit., Chapter 8, p. 215.

20. Foxall, op. cit. In his earlier observations on continuity in innovation,

he refers to T. S. Robertson, 'The Process of Innovation and the Diffusion of Innovations', *Journal of Marketing*, Vol. 3, No. 1, 1967, pp. 14–19.

21. R. H. Hayes and W. J. Abernathy, 'Managing our Way to Economic Decline' in Tushman and Moore (eds.), *Readings in the Management of Innovation* (op. cit.), Introduction (table reproduced from p. 19).

22. Mariann Jelinek, *Institutionalizing Innovation*, Praeger, New York, 1979, Introduction, p. xv.

23. R. Heller, 'The Legend of Litton' in Ansoff (ed.), *Business Strategy* (op. cit.), p. 366 (reprinted from *Management Today*, October 1967, pp. 60–67).

24. In a somewhat different context – of administrative change in government – Sir Douglass Wass, formerly Joint Head of the Home Civil Service in Britain, observes that: 'Years of experience have taught me to value the small steps along the right road above the great leap forward in the dark. In his essay "On Compromise," written just over a century ago, John Morley described the wise innovator as the man who had learned how to seize the chance of a small improvement while working incessantly in the direction of greater ones' (Wass, *Government and the Governed*, BBC Reith Lectures 1983, Routledge and Kegan Paul, London, 1984, Lecture 6, p. 118).

25. Gold, op. cit., p. 398.

Chapter 7: The politics of organization

1. Quoted in Margaret R. Thiele, *None but the Nightingale*, Charles E. Tuttle Company, Rutland, Vermont and Tokyo, 1967, Chapter VI, p. 55. She in turn ascribes it to Bynner, Witter (reprinted from *The Way of Life: According to Lao Tzu*, John Day Company, New York, 1944).

2. This is discussed succinctly in a short book by David Bradley and Roy Wilkie, *The Concept of Organization*, Blackie, Glasgow and London, 1974. See especially Chapter 3.

3. Kenneth J. Arrow, *The Limits of Organization*, Norton, New York, 1974, Chapter 2, p. 33.

4. James G. March and Herbert A. Simon, *Organizations*, Wiley, New York, 1958.

5. Arrow, op. cit., p. 33.

6. March and Simon, op. cit., Chapter 1, p. 4.

7. H. E. Norton, *Response to Rapid Change in Business*, lecture to final year B.Com. students at Birmingham University, 3 May 1983. Unpublished:

quoted by kind permission. Mr Norton was at that time Director of Planning at British Petroleum.

8. Wilfred Brown's view is put in this way by D. S. Pugh, D. J. Hickson and C. R. Hinings in *Writers on Organizations*, Penguin Books, Harmondsworth, second edition, 1971, 1 (Wilfred Brown), p. 72.

9. R. Monsen and A. Downs, 'A Theory of Large Managerial Firms' in Michael Gilbert (ed.), *The Modern Business Enterprise*, Penguin Books, Harmondsworth, 1972, 16, p. 352 (reprinted from *Journal of Political Economy*, Vol. 73, 1965, pp. 221–36).

10. Richard H. Hall, *Organizations: Structure and Process*, Prentice-Hall International Inc., London, 1974, pp. 85–6.

11. Hall, op. cit., pp. 86–7.

12. A. L. Minkes and R. H. Willis-Lee, 'Decision-Making in Organizations: Themes from a University Experience', *Education Journal*, Chinese University of Hong Kong, Vol. 13, No. 2, December 1985.

13. Arrow, op. cit., Chapter 3, p. 49.

14. Simon, *Administrative Behavior*, Chapter VIII, p. 156.

15. K. Boulding, 'The organization as a party to conflict' in John M. Thomas and Wassen G. Bennis (eds.), *Management of Change and Conflict*, Penguin Books, Harmondsworth, 1972, 15, p. 401 (reprinted from *Conflict and Defense*, Harper and Row, New York, 1963, pp. 145–65).

16. L. B. Curzon, in his chapter in 'Communication' cited earlier, gives these quotations. The first is from A. Bavelas and D. Barrett, 'An Experimental Approach to Organisational Communication' in L. W. Porter and K. Roberts (eds.), *Communication in Organizations*, Penguin Books, Harmondsworth, 1977; the second from Drucker, *Management*.

17. William P. Kennedy and Peter L. Payne, 'Directions for Future Research' in Leslie Hannah (ed.), *Management Strategy & Business Development*, Macmillan, London and Basingstoke, 1976, pp. 238–9.

18. Philip Selznick, *Leadership in Administration: A Sociological Interpretation*, Harper and Row, New York, Chapter 2, p. 63.

19. Andrew M. Pettigrew, *The Politics of Organizational Decision-Making*, Tavistock, London, in association with Van Gorcum, Assen, 1973, Chapter 2, p. 17.

20. Bradley and Wilkie, op. cit., Chapter 4, p. 56.

21. Henry Maddick and E. P. Pritchard, 'The Conventions of Local Authorities in the West Midlands', *Public Administration*, Parts I and II, Summer 1958 and 1959 respectively, *passim*. They refer to several usages of the term 'conventions' of government, which are essentially 'practices which are added

to those prescribed by law, and are adopted simply because they are found useful' (see Part I, p. 145).

See also Minkes and Nuttall, *Business Behaviour and Management Structure* (op. cit.), especially pp. 77–9.

Chapter 8: Strategy and planning

1. H. Igor Ansoff, *Corporate Strategy*, McGraw-Hill, New York, 1965.

Kenneth R. Andrews, *The Concept of Corporate Strategy*, Dow Jones-Irwin, 1971. References in this book are to the revised edition: Richard D. Irwin, Homewood, Illinois, 1980. Andrews had expressed his ideas earlier in a book he wrote with Learned, Christensen, and Guth, *Business Policy: Text and Cases*, Richard D. Irwin, 1965.

2. Charles W. Hofer and Dan Schendel, in *Strategy Formulation: Analytical Concepts*, West Publishing Company, St Paul, Minnesota, 1978, observe that Ansoff 'never formally defined what he meant by the term strategy' (see p. 17, text and note 6). Whether this is so or not, they take comments Ansoff makes in *Corporate Strategy* to mean that he saw it as 'the "common thread" among an organization's activities and product markets that defined the essential nature of the business that the organization was in and planned to be in in the future.'

3. Conversation with the author in 1981. Mr Fung was speaking of his policy framework and strategic decisions (two aspects which, as the later discussion in this chapter shows, can merge into each other).

4. Andrews, *The Concept of Corporate Strategy*, Chapter 2, p. 18.

5. Hofer and Schendel, op. cit., Chapter 1, p. 4.

6. Hofer and Schendel, ibid.

7. A. S. Mackintosh, *The Development of Firms*, Cambridge University Press, 1963.

On the wider definitional points, there is an interesting discussion in John Friend, 'The Dynamics of Policy Adjustment and Design in an Inter-Corporate Field', Preprint series of the International Institute of Management, Berlin, August 1975.

8. Edith Penrose, *The Theory of the Growth of the Firm*, Blackwell, Oxford, first edition, 1963, *passim*, but see especially pp. 46–9.

There is an interesting discussion of the idea of 'competence' in Selznick's *Leadership in Administration* (op. cit.).

9. Andrews, op. cit., Chapter 1.

10. James B. Quinn, *Strategies for Change: Logical Incrementalism*, Irwin, Homewood, Illinois, 1980, Chapter 4, p. 143.

11. Bernard W. E. Alford, 'The Chandler Thesis – Some General Observations' in Hannah (ed.), *Management Strategy and Business Development* (op. cit.). Alford here introduces the term 'diffused entrepreneurship', referred to elsewhere in this book.

12. Joseph L. Bower, 'On the Amoral Organization' in Robin Marris (ed.), *The Corporate Society*, Macmillan, London and Basingstoke, 1974, Chapter 6, pp. 196 and 199.

13. A good deal of research now includes study of managers' own perceptions of the strategic process in their organizations. The idea of strategy as a 'diffused' process also has implications for management education.

14. K. J. Arrow, 'Control in Large Organizations', *Management Science*, Vol. 10, No. 3, April 1964, p. 398.

15. Frank T. Cary, 'Management – The Key Resource', *The First Susan Yuen Memorial Lecture*, The Hong Kong Management Association, Hong Kong, 20 September 1985.

16. Alfred J. Chandler, Jr, 'The Development of Modern Management Structure in the US and UK' in Hannah (ed.), *Management Strategy and Business Development* (op. cit.).

17. A. L. Minkes and D. G. Tucker, 'J. A. Crabtree: A Pioneer of Business Management', *Business History*, Vol. XXI, No. 2, July 1979, p. 203.

18. Quinn, op. cit.

19. Quinn, ibid., Chapter 2, p. 58.

20. Quinn, ibid., Chapter 5, p. 205.

Chapter 9: Planning in the business corporation

1. Peter Hall, *Great Planning Disasters*, Penguin Books, Harmondsworth, 1981, Chapter 1, pp. 1 and 2.

2. Russell L. Ackoff, *A Concept of Corporate Planning*, John Wiley and Sons, New York, 1970, Chapter 1, p. 1.

3. Peter Lorange and Richard F. Vancil, 'How to design a strategic planning system', *Harvard Business Review* reprints of selected articles, *Planning*: Part V, p. 5. The paper originally appeared in *HBR*, September–October 1976.

4. R. H. Coase, 'The Nature of the Firm', *Economica*, New Series, Vol. IV, 1937; reprinted in *Readings in Price Theory*, American Economic Association, George Allen and Unwin, London, 1953, pp. 331–51.

5. A. J. Chandler, Jr, *The Visible Hand*, Harvard University Press, Cambridge, Massachusetts, 1977. Arrow, *The Limits of Organization* (op. cit.), p. 25.

6. Mr Saxon Tate, managing director of Tate and Lyle at the time, made this comment in a conversation at Birmingham University.

Size of units and of headquarters staff exercises the minds of top executives; so do the related topics of centralization and decentralization. Richard Young, formerly assistant managing director, and Roy Bagnall, formerly joint managing director of Tube Investments, were among those who discussed the topics (see Minkes and Nuttall, *Business Behaviour and Management Structure*, pp. 66–8). They were interested in the questions of channels of communication, strategic control and operational devolution.

7. David W. Ewing (ed.), *Long-Range Planning for Management*, Harper and Row, New York, third edition 1972, Parts 1 and 2.

8. D. W. Ewing, 'The Time Dimension' in Ewing (ed.), op. cit., Chapter 37, p. 450.

9. H. I. Ansoff, 'The Firm of the Future' in Ansoff (ed.), *Business Strategy* (op. cit.), p. 120 (reprinted from *Harvard Business Review*, September–October 1965).

10. R. I. Tricker, *Corporate Governance*, Gower, Aldershot, 1984, Chapter 5, p. 54, and Chapter 6, p. 80.

11. Lorange and Vancil, op. cit.

12. R. L. Ackoff, 'The Systems Revolution' in Martin Lockett and Roger Spear (eds.), *Organizations as Systems*, Open University, Milton Keynes, 1980. Figure 5 is based on Ackoff's analysis on pp. 30–32. The reading is drawn from 'The Systems Revolution', *Long Range Planning*, Vol. 7, No. 6, December 1974, pp. 2–5, and 'Resurrecting the Future of Operational Research', *Journal of the Operational Research Society*, Vol. 30, No. 3, pp. 189–93 (both Pergamon Press).

13. Figure 6 is reproduced from Ansoff, *Corporate Strategy*, Chapter 10, p. 221.

14. L. B. Curzon, *Teaching in Further Education*, Holt, Rinehart and Wilson, London, third edition, 1985, Chapter 10, p. 112.

15. Lorange and Vancil, op. cit.

16. Ackoff, op. cit., p. 31.

17. Tricker, op. cit., Chapter 10, pp. 173–4.

18. K. K. Tse, *Marks and Spencer*, Pergamon Press, Oxford, 1985, Introduction, p. 9.

19. R. F. Vancil and P. Lorange, 'Strategic Planning in Diversified Companies', *Harvard Business Review*, January–February 1981, p. 81. See R. N. Paul, N. B. Donovan, J. W. Taylor, 'The Reality Gap in Strategic Planning', *Harvard Business Review* reprints, *Planning* (op. cit.), p. 5.

20. The report on which this summary of the conference is based appeared in *The Economist*, 5 November 1983, p. 81.

21. Hall, op. cit., Chapter 6, p. 138.

22. From a paper of the Early Warning Group, quoted by kind permission of Sir Adrian Cadbury. In one of it meetings in 1980, for example, the group considered attitude groupings in the UK population, trends in medicine and health care and in the desire for knowledge about nutrition, and changes in attitudes towards the home.

23. Quinn, op. cit., pp. 39–40.

Chapter 10: What about non-market organizations?

1. Richard M. Cyert, *The Management of Nonprofit Organizations*, D. C. Heath, Lexington, Massachusetts, 1975, Essay 1, p. 7. This book contains lectures by Cyert with responses by a number of other contributors. It is subtitled 'With Emphasis on Universities', but has some wider implications.

2. J. G. March (ed.), *Handbook of Organizations*, Rand McNally, Chicago, 1965, Introduction, p. ix.

3. Ronald C. Bauer, *Cases in College Administration*, Bureau of Publications, Teachers College, Columbia University, New York, 1955.

4. The author is indebted to Dr R. H. Willis-Lee for helpful comments on topics discussed in this section. The passages dealing with nationalized industries are substantially based on A. L. Minkes, 'Nationalised industries in retrospect', *Journal of General Management*, Vol. 11, No. 1, Autumn 1985, pp. 29–37.

Neither the references to postal business in this section nor the information and discussion in it derive from the author's experience as a member of the Midlands Postal Board (1974–80).

5. M. J. Daunton, *Royal Mail: The Post Office Since 1840*, Athlone Press, London and Dover, New Hampshire, 1985, Chapter 10, p. 351.

6. R. Kenneth McGeorge, 'Case Mix Management Systems' in John M. Virgo (ed.), *Exploring New Vistas in Health Care*, International Health Economics and Management Institute, Edwardsville, Illinois, 1985, Chapter 19, p. 218.

7. Jeffrey E. Harris, 'The internal organization of hospitals: some economic implications', *The Bell Journal of Economics*, Vol. 8, No. 2, Autumn 1977, pp. 467–82.

8. Harris, ibid., p. 469.

9. Daniel S. Cochran, Mel Schnake, and Ron Earl, 'Effect of Organiza-

tional Size on Conflict Frequency and Location in Hospitals', *Journal of Management Studies*, Vol. 20, No. 4, October 1983, p. 442.

10. Harris, op. cit., p. 478.

11. Charles Perrow, 'Hospitals: Technology, Structure, and Goals' in March (ed.), *Handbook of Organizations* (op. cit.), Chapter 23, p. 914.

12. Allan Warmington, 'Organisation Theory and Health Service Admini- stration' in David Allen and James A. Hughes (eds.), *Management for Health Service Administrators*, Pitman, London and Massachusetts, 1983.

13. The first part of this section draws on A. L. Minkes and R. H. Willis- Lee, 'Decision-Making in Organizations: Themes from a University Ex- perience', *Education Journal*, Chinese University of Hong Kong, Vol. 13, No. 2, December 1985, pp. 79–89.

14. Robert Aitken, *Administration of a University*, University of London Press, 1966.

15. Minkes and Willis-Lee, op. cit.

16. On the wider question of the concept of marketing in non-business contexts, see Gordon Foxall, 'Marketing's Domain', *European Journal of Marketing*, Vol. 18, No. 1, 1984.

17. Lotte Bailyn, 'Autonomy in the Industry R and D Lab', *Human Resource Management*, Vol. 24, Number 2, Summer 1985, p. 132.

18. R. H. Hall, 'Professional/Management Relations: Imagery vs. Action', *Human Resource Management*, Vol. 24, No. 2, Summer 1985, p. 228.

19. Bailyn, op. cit., p. 133.

20. Cyert, op. cit.

Chapter 11: Themes for the future

1. A. P. Sloan, *My Years with General Motors*, Sidgwick and Jackson, London, 1965, *passim*.

2. Stewart, *The Reality of Management* (op. cit.), Introduction, p. 10.

3. Leonardo da Vinci, MS. B4V, quoted by Anna Maria Brizio, 'The Words of Leonardo' in Carlo Zammattio, Augusto Marinoni, Anna Maria Brizio, *Leonardo the Scientist* , McGraw Hill, Maidenhead, 1980.

4. Stewart, op. cit.

5. G. A. H. Cadbury, 'Our Technological Future', *The Institution of Production Engineers. The 1969 Viscount Nuffield Memorial Lecture*, given at the University of Leicester, 29 October 1969, p. 11.

6. J. L. Bower, *The Two Faces of Management*, Houghton Mifflin, Boston, 1983, Chapter 2, p. 40.

7. Cadbury, op. cit., p. 11.

INDEX